ATTITUDE VOLUME 1

Wholeness and Holiness

32 Powerful Sessions on Real-Life Issues for Teens

Living the Good News
a division of Church Publishing Incorporated
Editorial Offices
600 Grant Street, Suite 400
Denver, CO 80203

James R. Creasey, Publisher

Graphic Design and Illustration: Carolyn Klass

Project Editor: Dirk deVries

Writers: Dirk deVries, Kathy Mulhern, Rachel Gluckstern, Nate Faudel, Jerry Berg, Jessie Duvall, Lesley Friis, Matt Skeen, Jessica Kirk, Jared Crain, Lori VanDeman

Printed in the United States of America.

The scripture quotations used herein are from the Today's English Version — Second Edition, ©1992 American Bible Society. Used by permission.

ISBN 1-889108-42-1

CONTENTS

INTRODUCTION

Who are these teens with whom (and for whom) we work? Just when we think we've pegged them, they surprise us—and *surprise* may be an understatement—by saying something so profound (or not!) or doing something so compassionate (or not!)—that we're back to ground zero, at a loss for an appropriate response. As an editor (and former youth worker) with a particular interest in serving this diverse demographic, I continue to ask the questions, read the statistics, expose myself to the media that appeal to teens and embody their interests, values and dreams. Who *are* they? What do they seek? What motivates them? hurts them? confuses them? comforts them? angers them? guides them?

But I've decided, recently, that though the questions I'm asking have value, and the answers I'm finding are helpful, there's something slightly misguided about them all: I'm asking too many questions *about* teenagers and not nearly enough questions *of* teenagers.

So, with ATTITUDE (Volume One of which you now hold in your hands) I *started* with teens. I gathered a group of diverse teenagers and asked, "So what would *you* want to do if you were to meet together with other teens in a church setting? What would make that time worthwhile? What would you want to talk about? What would help you focus in on these topics? What resources would you use? What approaches would you take?"

Their responses both moved and challenged me. I was moved by the breadth and depth of their concerns: love, God, prayer, prejudice, dating, health, jealousy, sex, parents, siblings, AIDS, aging, rejection, work, marriage, death, anger, fear, friendship, etc.

I was challenged by this: "Don't ask for our input unless you're serious about letting us do it the way we believe is best; don't patronize us by editing what we say into what you think we should have said or how we should have done it."

Yikes!

And so I (as an editor) and we (as a company) take a risk, offering a resource that truly allows teens to engage other teens on their own terms, inviting them to bring their authentic selves into an encounter with both scripture and the shared traditions of our faith. Some of the questions they ask in this process are tougher ones than we might have asked; some of the topics tread on territory we would rather not cover; some of the articles express unorthodox opinions; many activities ask questions that invite participants to draw their own conclusions, without providing canned answers.

Out of respect for the teens involved in this process—as well as respect for teens who will benefit from the result of that process—we present a resource that flows directly from their experience; we let their personalities and perspectives come through in the pages that follow. We choose to trust the hearts, minds *and faith* of teens.

I invite you to take that risk, too. The hundreds of teens who have already used this resource in various forms confirm that the approach works. We believe the risk is worth it. We believe teens relate immediately and powerfully to a resource that so closely echoes their experiences.

This volume of ATTITUDE provides thirty-two session plans dealing with various aspects of personal growth, both emotional and spiritual. Depending on the size and nature of your group, as well as how the session is conducted, each session plan provides enough material for 45-75 minutes. Each two-page session plan is followed by an accompanying, reproducible handout. For each session, each group member will need a copy of the corresponding handout, folded to form a four-page paper. (When photocopying, please respect the guidelines described on the copyright and permissions page.)

Your use of ATTITUDE is only limited by your imagination (and that of the teens in your group or class—remember to solicit their input). Here are a few suggestions:

● *For weekly or bi-weekly youth meetings.* For example, help teens develop a closer relationship with God by first using the four sessions on "Growing Closer to God" (pp. 103-118) and then the four sessions on "Questions of Faith" (pp. 119-134).

● *For day-long or weekend retreats:* Build a retreat around four or more ATTITUDE sessions; either focus on a single topic (like "Transitions," pp. 55-70), or choose from all three volumes of ATTITUDE, assembling topics of interest to your group members.

● *For religious education:* Substitute or supplement a regular religious education session (in the parish or in the school) with an ATTITUDE topic of immediate relevance; for example, cover "Dedicating Yourself to God" (pp. 63-66) close to confirmation, "Divorce" (pp. 55-58) when the parents of a group member have decided to split, or "Anger" (pp. 31-34) when group members are having trouble getting along.

● *For special events:* Rely on ATTITUDE for special-event programming, like a parent-teen night (try using "Becoming an Adult," pp. 87-90) or an ice-cream social with teens and parish retirees (try using "Aging," pp. 99-102).

To find ATTITUDE sessions dealing with specific topics or selected scriptures, see the indexes at the back of the book (pp. 135-136). You'll note that the indexes cover all three volumes in the ATTITUDE series.

The teenage writers of ATTITUDE intend the sessions to be led by teens as much as by adult leaders; involve your class or group members in both choosing topics and facilitating meetings.

So who *are* these teenagers whom we love and lead? Ask *them.* Listen to, respect and learn from their answers. You, too, may be both surprised and challenged by what you hear.

Dirk deVries
Editorial Co-Director
Living the Good News

LEADER'S GUIDE

FOCUS

Emotions: Insecurity

SCRIPTURE

Luke 15:1-7

SCAN

Today's meeting explores the painful feeling of insecurity:
● In Attitude Check, volunteers use movement to reflect strong emotions, including insecurity.
● Attitude Question examines the experience of insecurity.
● Attitude Exit looks to the teaching of Jesus for assurance of our value.
● In Attitude Adjustment, group members share affirmations as an antidote to insecurity.
● In Attitude Exit, members create the first of four scripture "tools" to help handle strong emotions.

STUFF

Bibles
photocopies of today's paper (pp. 9-10), 1 per group member
pens or pencils
colored construction paper
colored felt markers
scissors
slips of paper
paper lunch bags, 1 per group member
assorted craft materials: glue, scissors, glitter, stickers, ribbon, googly eyes, etc.

1. Attitude Check: EMOTION WALK

Recruit a volunteer for an "emotion walk." Explain to the volunteer:
● Walk the length of the room.
● As you walk, let your body—your face, your posture and the way you walk—reflect the feelings that I call out.

As the volunteer walks, call out these and other feelings:
● anger
● love
● loneliness
● happiness
● hate
● fear

Repeat with other volunteers and other feelings, then ask several volunteers to walk the room together while group members call out feelings. Encourage members who are calling out feelings to allow several seconds between suggested feelings.

Finally, ask the *entire* group to walk the room as you alone call out feelings. Name two or three feelings, then say one final feeling, *insecurity*. Allow group members to reflect insecurity for a longer period of time.

2. Attitude Question: WHY DO I FEEL SO INSECURE?

Discuss:
● How did we reflect the final feeling, insecurity? What did we do with our faces? our bodies? the way we walked?
● How do people reflect insecurity in the way they talk?
● Where do we see insecurity in other people at home? at school? on the street? among our friends?
● When do we see insecurity within ourselves?
● Where do feelings of insecurity come from?
  — With which people or in which situations do we feel most insecure?
  — With which people or in which situations do we feel most secure?
  — What makes the difference between feeling secure and feeling insecure?

- Some say that *all* people feel insecure. Do you agree or disagree? Explain.
- How do you think God feels about our feelings of insecurity? What do you imagine might be God's answer to insecurity?
- Let's take a look at one answer to insecurity in today's Attitude Search.

3. Attitude Search: LUKE 15:1-7

Distribute Bibles and invite group members to turn to Luke 15:1-7. Ask a volunteer to read aloud this passage.

After the reading, divide participants into small groups of 3-4 members each. Explain to groups:
- In your small group, think of another way to tell Jesus' parable of the lost sheep.
- You could, for example, tell about a child lost in a mall, a pet caught in a thunderstorm or a teenager kicked out of the house and living on the street.
- Be ready to tell your new parable to the full group.

Give small groups time to prepare, then regather and ask one group to tell its new parable. After the parable, ask:
- How does it feel to be a lost...*(insert the lost person or object used by the group)?*
- When in our lives do we feel lost like this?
- What's the greatest hope of a lost... *(insert the lost person or object)?*
- How does such a lost...*(person or object)* discover that he *(or she or it)* is valued? cared for? loved?

Ask other groups to share their parables, repeating the questions for each. Conclude by asking:
- How does God seek us out like lost sheep?

4. Attitude Adjustment: STAR BAGS

Seat group members in a circle. Distribute a pen or pencil and a paper bag to each group member. Make available the craft materials, slips of paper, construction paper and felt markers. Explain:
- Create a Star Bag for the person seated to your left.
- Label the bag with the person's name. Decorate the bag as you wish using the available craft materials.
- When you've finished your bag, write an affirmation for every person in the group on a separate slip of paper.

Place the completed bags in the center of the room. Ask group members to drop their affirmation slips into the appropriate bags.

Have each individual retrieve the bag created for him or her. Ask group members to read *only one* of the slips inside at this time. Explain that they may take the bags home and read the remaining affirmations later.

5. Attitude Exit: A TOOL AND A BLESSING

Distribute photocopies of today's ATTITUDE paper and invite group members to complete the activity This Week's Tool, printed in the papers.

When they have finished, stand together in a circle and invite volunteers to share and explain the tool they've chosen.

Close by offering blessings for each other, perhaps asking each group member to offer a blessing for the person on his or her right. Group members could repeat this blessing or offer one of their own:
- *(Name of group member)*, this week, may God show you how incredibly valuable you are!

a division of
Church Publishing
Incorporated

600 Grant St., #400
Denver, CO 80203
1.800.824.1813

INSECURITY

ATTITUDE
FOR TEENS BY TEENS

THE COMPARISON GAME
by Jessie Duvall

If only we could read people's minds:

Sarah thinks, "I shouldn't be in this class. I'm not near as smart as everyone else in here..."

Mika thinks, "Sarah is so pretty. I wish I had her hair..."

Tom thinks, "So, should I ask Jenny out or what? She'll probably say no anyway. Why would she go out with me when she could have any guy she wants?"

Jenny thinks, "I wish Tom would ask me out. He's so cute. But why would he want to go out with me?"

Oh, well..."

Frank thinks, "I want to try out for the varsity soccer team, but I'm not sure how good I am compared to the other guys..."

Silvia thinks, "I wish I hadn't worn these jeans. I'm sure everyone is talking about how big my butt is..."

Can you relate? We all can.

Insecurity is a common, normal feeling. Fashion models feel it. World leaders feel it. Sports stars feel it.

(continued on page 4)

INSECURITY
by Rachel Gluckstern

Oh, wow, look at her!
I'll never look like that.
And look at her boyfriend.
I'll never get a guy like that.

Gee, look at her *grade!*
I'd love to get an A.
Look how the teacher is proud.
He'll never be proud of me.

Man, look at his *muscles!*
I could never be that strong.
And all those girls around him.
None of them would ever look at me.

Ever stop to think
You look at others too much?
Stop to look at yourself.
What good do you see there?

COMPARISON GAME *(continued from page 1)*

People feel insecure about their looks, their intelligence, their personality, their athletic ability...just about anything you can think of. The thoughts of the kids above echo my own. I'm sure they echo yours too.

I don't know of a secret way to end all insecurity. I do know it helps to avoid the comparison game. Constantly compare yourself to others and you'll focus on your "weaker" points and end up feeling lousy.

Chances are, most other people are so worried about their own insecurities that they won't even notice what you believe to be such obvious flaws in yourself.

You, like me, may not be the prettiest or the smartest or the most popular, but don't let that stop you from feeling good about yourself. You are so precious to God that "even the hairs of your head have all been counted" (Matthew 10:30).

After all, "If only the loveliest-sounding birds of the forest sang, it would be a very quiet place."

© Copyright 2000
Living the Good News
a division of Church Publishing Incorporated
600 Grant Street
Suite 400
Denver, CO 80203
1 (800) 824-1813

Graphic Design & Illustration:
Carolyn Klass

ATTITUDE

Living the Good News

THIS WEEK'S TOOL (FOR COPING WITH INSECURITY)

Create for yourself a "tool" to help you deal with feelings of insecurity this week. Here's how:

1 Cut a tool out of construction paper. A hammer, screwdriver, saw, whatever...

2 Choose a Bible verse or phrase to help you cope with insecurity. You could, for example, choose something from today's reading from Luke 15, like verse 4:

"Suppose one of you has a hundred sheep and loses one of them—what do you do? You leave the other ninety-nine sheep in the pasture and go looking for the one that got lost until you find it."

Or maybe this, which is in Psalm 139:

"You created every part of me; you put me together in my mother's womb."

Or choose a verse from one of these scriptures:

Romans 8:31-39
Psalm 23
1 Samuel 16:7
Psalm 46:1-3
Psalm 62:1-2

Or use a verse you find yourself!

3 Write your chosen phrase or verse on your construction-paper tool.

4 Use the tool throughout the week whenever you're feeling insecure. Let God encourage you through the words of scripture.

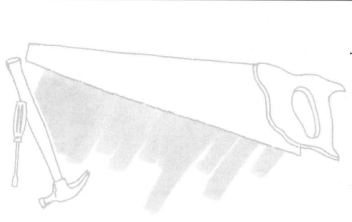

THE [___] INSIDE STORY

...every day God is looking for you.

LUKE 15:3-7

Jesus tells us a story about a lost sheep and a shepherd.

Imagine this commercial: "Lost sheep and their feelings of insecurity—on the next 'Oprah.'"

This might be the line of questioning during the interview: Why didn't you feel comfortable with the other sheep? Did you feel rejected? How did you feel when you were lost? How did you get lost in the first place? Weren't you paying attention? Where did you go? How did you feel when you realized all the others had gone on without you?

On "Oprah," it would all be about the sheep. Why? Because we're caught up in our lostness. We feel bad about not keeping up with the others. We're astonished and dismayed at our inability to fit in, at our feelings of not being good enough, at our failure to impress others with our looks or talents. Inside, we're wandering alone, wondering whether we're worth anything at all.

But the glorious focus of Jesus' story is the shepherd, not the sheep. The shepherd doesn't care about why or how the sheep wandered off. And it's not enough that he has ninety-nine other perfectly safe sheep. He has to have that one. That lost sheep is irreplaceable.

That's the way God feels about you. Even if everybody else was in the kingdom, God would go looking for you. God has gone looking for you. Even now, every day, God is looking for you.

Like the shepherd, God is not waiting for you to find your own way back. God is not holding off until you get your act together. If you're looking for God, God will run to gather you up. If you're stuck on a cliff, God will find a way to reach you. If you're hiding, God will discover you.

The shepherd wants you.

LEADER'S GUIDE

FOCUS

Emotions: Loneliness

SCRIPTURE

John 20:1-18

SCAN

In today's meeting, group members discuss ways to cope with loneliness:
● In Attitude Check, group members try to guess which roles are pinned to their backs.
● Attitude Question asks members to share personal stories of loneliness.
● Attitude Search tells the story of a woman experiencing overwhelming grief and loneliness.
● In Attitude Adjustment, group members share advice for coping with loneliness.
● Attitude Exit invites members to choose a scripture "tool" for coping with life's lonely times.

STUFF

Bibles
photocopies of today's paper (pp. 13-14), 1 per group member
colored construction paper
colored felt markers
scissors
safety pins
chalkboard and chalk or newsprint and marker

Before the meeting prepare sheets of construction paper on which you have written roles for today's Attitude Check. Write one role on each sheet. Suggested roles include: *beauty queen, jock, rebel, nerd, Casanova/playboy, flirt, smart Einstein type, someone with AIDS, politician, homeless person, wealthy person, druggie, elderly person, musician, Hare Krishna, drug dealer, prostitute, ex-convict, physically challenged person, etc.*

Add other roles of your own and feel free to repeat roles, if necessary, to be sure you have prepared one sheet for each participant.

1. Attitude Check: ONLY THE LONELY

As each group member arrives, pin to his or her back one of the sheets of construction paper prepared **before the meeting**. Be certain that members do not see the roles being pinned to their backs.

When all members have arrived, and a role is pinned to each back, explain:
● Treat each person in the group as if they are the person whose role is printed on his or her back.
● Each individual is to try to guess what's written on his or her back.

Give group members time to try to figure out who they are. When all roles have been guessed, remove the pins and papers and continue with Attitude Question.

2. Attitude Question: WHO ARE THE LONELY?

Discuss:
● In this game, who felt liked? accepted? popular? How were these people treated?
● Who felt lonely? shunned? unaccepted? unpopular? How were these people treated?
● When in our day-to-day lives do we feel the most lonely?
● What's the difference between being alone and feeling lonely?
  — When do we feel lonely, even in a group?
● Why do people experience loneliness?

ATTITUDE FOR TEENS BY TEENS

- Respond to this statement: *Everyone experiences loneliness.*
  — To what degree is this statement true?
  — How can this statement be an encouragement for those who feel lonely?

3. Attitude Search: JOHN 20:1-18

Distribute pens or pencils, Bibles and paper. Divide participants into groups of 4-5 members each. Offer groups these directions:
- In your small group, read aloud John 20:1-11a. Stop with the line that reads, "Mary stood crying outside the tomb."
- After you've finished reading, write a list of all the different feelings Mary probably experienced as she spends this time in the garden. What was she feeling in verses 1-11a?

Give groups time to complete their reading and their lists, then gather and ask:
- What feelings did you list? (*Ask a volunteer to record group members' responses on chalkboard or newsprint.*)
- Think of all that Jesus had meant to Mary. He may have been the first person to truly accept and love her, just as she was. Now it seemed he was gone forever.
- Which of the feelings we've just listed are a part of loneliness?
- When have you felt the kind of loneliness Mary feels in these verses?

Invite participants to return to their small groups. Continue:
- Now read John 20:11-18.
- When you've finished reading, write a list of all the different feelings Mary probably experienced in verses 11b-18.

When groups have finished, call members together and ask:
- Now what do you imagine Mary is feeling? (*Add these feelings to the list.*)

- What has changed the way Mary feels?
- How can the knowledge that Jesus is alive and with us help us to deal with our own feelings of loneliness?

4. Attitude Adjustment: ENCOURAGING THE LONELY

Introduce today's Attitude Adjustment by explaining:
- In this activity, we will suggest to each other ways to cope with loneliness.
- Just listening to suggestions may not help much, but of the dozens of suggestions we all hear, there may be a few that really do help.

Ask a volunteer to sit in the center of the group circle. Invite the volunteer to complete this statement:
- I feel loneliest when...

After the volunteer has completed the statement, give each group member an opportunity to respond to the volunteer's completed statement with a way to cope with the lonely situation named by the volunteer. Repeat with other volunteers.

5. Attitude Exit: A TOOL AND A BLESSING

Distribute photocopies of today's ATTITUDE paper and invite group members to complete the activity This Week's Tool, printed in the papers.

When they have finished, invite volunteers to share the tool they've created.

Close by offering blessings to each other. Group members may use this blessing or one of their own:
- May God remain close to you this week, when you feel loved and accepted, but especially when you feel lonely.

a division of Church Publishing Incorporated

600 Grant St., #400
Denver, CO 80203
1.800.824.1813

LONELINESS

ATTITUDE
BY TEENS FOR TEENS

THE WAY IT FEELS by Rachel Gluckstern

You walk through the halls, never looking to the side. You avoid eye contact. In class, you sit quietly, perhaps ignoring everyone in the room and escaping into your book.

Or maybe you're the most popular person in school. You strut down the halls, saying Hi to everyone and anyone. You're the last and the loudest to get to class.

And you are an incredibly lonely person.

The first example is the stereotype: quiet, withdrawn, shy. No one who was popular could ever be this lonely, right?

Actually, someone might be popular and outgoing *because* they are lonely. They make themselves known because inside they are scared that if they're not the center of attention, they'll lose all recognition and be friendless. They fear invisibility most of all.

Sometimes popular people are lonely because they have not been true to themselves, and, as a result, no one really knows them. It's lonely to be accepted for your facade, not for your real self.

Whatever its cause and however we cope with it, overwhelming

(continued on page 2)

CHANGING by Lesley Friis

Melissa has it all: long, blond hair, understanding parents, nice home. All day long friends surround her, eating lunch, sitting in class or hanging around after school.

Yes, Melissa has it all...including loneliness.

Melissa feels lonely because the real Melissa is hidden. Sure, she has friends, but with none of them can she share her innermost thoughts. She's just Melissa, being there, going along, talking some (but not much), never asserting herself, never expressing her opinion, just agreeing and accompanying. They let her be with them.

But none of them knows her.

Melissa's ready to start being who she is. She wants to tell others what she feels and experiences. Melissa wants someone to compare notes on life with. With her friends she sometimes thinks, Stop! Listen to me! But she never says it aloud.

She knows it's not their fault. She wonders where they learned to simply be who they are. Who taught them to ask for what they wanted? Why was it okay for them to say how they felt? why they were angry? what made them happy? And why can't she do the same thing?

It takes a lot of courage, but one day, in the middle of a frustrating day, while eating lunch with her friends, Melissa blurts out, "I feel so lonely, you guys!"

And it is a beginning...

© Copyright 2000
Living the Good News
a division of Church Publishing Incorporated
600 Grant Street
Suite 400
Denver, CO 80203
1 (800) 824-1813

Graphic Design & Illustration:
Carolyn Klass

ATTITUDE

Living the Good News

THIS WEEK'S TOOL [FOR COPING WITH LONELINESS]

Create for yourself a "tool" to help you deal with lonely times this week. Here's how:

1 Cut a tool out of construction paper—a hammer, screwdriver, saw, whatever. If you made a tool in the last ATTITUDE session, make a different one now.

2 Look up several of these scriptures and choose a phrase or verse as your tool for coping with loneliness this week. Each offers encouragement for lonely times:

> Romans 8:38-39
> Matthew 28:18-20 (especially the end of verse 20)
> John 14:16-17
> 2 Corinthians 1:3-4
> Psalm 25:15-18

3 Copy your chosen scripture phrase or verse on your construction-paper tool.

4 Use the tool throughout the week whenever you're feeling lonely. God can encourage you through the words of scripture.

THE WAY IT FEELS (continued from page 1)

loneliness can be dangerous. Loneliness can lead us to make desperate choices to relieve our feelings of lonely worthlessness. Some people use drugs, sex or alcohol. Others withdraw and cut off all friendships. A few choose suicide.

Everyone will feel lonely now and then. This is a part of life. If you feel lonely all the time, tell someone. If you feel lonely and unloved, remember that God loves you and eagerly listens to you; God supports you in your hard times.

And be who you really are. Openness and authenticity—being real—attracts friends.

It's easy to feel lonely in a crowded world. Choose an alternative: reach out for help.

JOHN 20:1-18

Loneliness is not an uncommon problem. In fact, it has undoubtedly been experienced by every person in all of human history. The problem, of course, is made worse by the fact that we must bear loneliness alone, which makes us feel like no one else out there could understand or help.

We may have lots of friends, even very close friends, and still feel lonely. We may be the most popular person at every weekend party, but still feel lonely.

Loneliness is a very small, but very deep, empty space down in the furthest reaches of our hearts. And though our day-to-day lives are full of good things and great friends, every once in a while we all hear echoes from that empty space. Echoes that speak of abandonment or friendlessness or rejection. We're lonely because we know that there's an inner core of who we are that we are unable to share with anyone.

Mary Magdalene fell right into that deep empty space in her heart when she lost Jesus twice. It broke her heart when her friend was tortured and executed. But the final blow—the disappearance of his body when she was looking for some comfort in touching it, anointing it, lovingly preparing it for burial—pitched her into the emptiness.

But then Jesus speaks her name. In the darkest and most empty place in her heart, Mary found Jesus waiting for her. He called her up and out of her loneliness. Then she knew that the next time she heard echoes from her place of loneliness, he would be there.

Because of Jesus' resurrection, Mary's experience is ours, too. When all the other voices of friendship in our lives are strangely still, and the emptiness that we call loneliness begins to beckon, Jesus will be there. And he calls us by name.

INSIDE STORY

> In the darkest and most empty place in her heart, Mary found Jesus waiting for her.

LEADER'S GUIDE

FOCUS

Emotions: Guilt

SCRIPTURE

1 John 1:5-10

SCAN

Today's meeting examines both true guilt, which calls us to confession and forgiveness, and false guilt, which unnecessarily robs us of freedom and joy:

- In Attitude Check, group members compete in a Guilt-Trip Contest.
- In Attitude Question, group members discuss the difference between true and false guilt.
- Attitude Search provides a biblical measure for distinguishing true and false guilt.
- Attitude Adjustment invites small groups to practice a helpful strategy for coping with false guilt.
- In Attitude Exit, members are reminded of God's provision for true guilt.

STUFF

Bibles
photocopies of today's paper (pp. 17-18), 1 per group member
chalkboard and chalk or newsprint and marker
colored construction paper
colored felt markers
scissors

1. Attitude Check: GUILT-TRIP CONTEST

Welcome participants and divide them into two teams. Explain:

- Within your team, think up really good guilt-trip statements, comments designed to make others feel guilty.

- You can use statements you've heard before or those you create yourselves.
- Teams will alternate saying their statements, trying to create a feeling of guilt in the other team.
- Remember, the look on the face and the tone of voice as these lines are delivered can greatly add to their guilt-producing impact.

If group members would like examples of guilt-trip statements, offer these "true-life" examples:

- It's up to you, but *I* wouldn't do it.
- You're never home. You never talk to us. We never see you any more.
- But Wednesday night is our family night!

Throughout the contest, have a volunteer write down all guilt-trip statements on a separate sheet of newsprint or another section of the chalkboard. These will be used in Attitude Adjustment.

Conduct the contest as interest and time allow. Ask teams to decide which team presented the best guilt-producing statements. Continue with Attitude Question.

2. Attitude Question: WHEN IS GUILT REAL?

Ask group members to sit in a circle. Discuss:

- Define *guilt*.
- What does guilt feel like?
- How do you know when you feel guilty?
- How do you know when a friend feels guilty?
- What is real or true guilt?
  — When is feeling guilty appropriate?
  — What should real or true guilt lead us to do?
  — In what ways can guilt work in your life for the good?
  — What do you think God wants us to do about true guilt?

ATTITUDE FOR TEENS BY TEENS

● What is false guilt?
  — At what times is feeling guilty inappropriate? harmful?
  — In what ways do people use guilt to get what they want? to communicate without being upfront and honest?
  — What do you think God wants us to do about false guilt?

3. Attitude Search: 1 JOHN 1:5-10

Distribute Bibles and ask a volunteer to read aloud 1 John 1:5-7. Discuss:
● What do you think John means when he says that God is light?
● John says there is no darkness in God. Give examples of "darkness."
● Give examples of ways in which we might live in darkness, as John mentions.
● Why is it impossible to both live in darkness and have fellowship with God?
● Give examples of ways in which we live in the light.
● How does John say we can know when we're living in the light?
● What happens to our "true guilt" when we live in the light?

Ask another volunteer to read aloud 1 John 1:8-10. Discuss:
● What provision has God made for our true guilt?

Distribute copies of today's ATTITUDE paper and invite group members to read silently The Inside Story, printed in the papers. Discuss:
● What simple principle does John give to help us determine false from true guilt? *("Does your behavior intensify your fellowship with God? If it does...you are not guilty. If your behavior breaks that fellowship, then you are guilty of sin.")*
● When in your life can this principle help you let go of false guilt? deal with true guilt?

4. Attitude Adjustment: LETTING GO OF GUILT

Divide into small groups. Make sure all groups can see the chalkboard or newsprint on which you listed the guilt-trip producers in Attitude Check.

Ask each group to use this form to explore each of the items listed in Attitude Check:
● They say...*(insert statement from Attitude Check)...*
● ...but what they really mean is...*(restate what the statement from Attitude Check is really intending...)*

Example:
● They say, "You're never home,"
● but what they really mean is, "I miss you and I'm afraid you're growing up and won't be my little boy/girl any more."

Give groups time to experiment with this formula, then regather and ask:
● How did this exercise help us understand the motivation behind common "guilt trips"?
● How has this exercise equipped us to better handle guilt trips in the future?

5. Attitude Exit: A TOOL AND A BLESSING

Invite group members individually to complete the activity This Week's Tool, printed in today's ATTITUDE paper.

Ask volunteers to share and explain the tools they've chosen.

Close by offering a blessing to each other. Group members may use this blessing or one of their own:
● May God grant you forgiveness for true guilt and release from false guilt.

Living the Good News

a division of Church Publishing Incorporated

600 GRANT ST., #400
DENVER, CO 80203
1.800.824.1813

GUILT

ATTITUDE
FOR TEENS BY TEENS

FORGIVENESS, THE ULTIMATE CURE FOR GUILT
by Matt Skeen

Ten seconds after, he regretted it.

That night was even worse.

Steve had stolen the school's pride and joy—the lion sculpture in the school entry. The lion embodied their school spirit, the spirit that had made them state champions. Now it sat, out of place, in a corner of his basement, awkwardly staring at him with large solemn eyes, reprimanding him. Steve covered it with an old sheet, went to his room and fell into a restless, uneasy sleep.

On the way to school in the morning, the friends who had dared him laughed and congratulated him on his risky stunt. But the uproar at school cut short his moment of glory. No one knew who had done it, and it was a good thing for Steve: the perpetrator was in deep waters with both the administration and, even worse, the other students.

Steve went home sick later in the day. Kneeling on the floor of the basement, Steve could feel the lion's eyes watching him through the sheet. "Please, God," Steve prayed, "forgive me. I'm going to take it back right now." He hefted the lion and struggled up the basement stairs.

Two days later, the guilt still lingered. Every few hours he'd be aware of the dark cloud hanging over him and he'd ask God for forgiveness once again. The feeling of guilt stayed.

Finally, Steve called his youth pastor, Tonya. He told her the story, hoping that confessing once again would help relieve his conscience.

"Steve," Tonya said quietly, "if you've asked God for forgiveness, then it's done."

"Done?"

"The guilt you now feel is not from God. It's your own holding on to what is over and done with. It's history. God's forgiven you. Can you do the same?"

Steve thought for a few seconds. "If God could do it, I guess I could too."

"I've got a favorite scripture in Philippians," Tonya said. "It's part of Philippians 3:13: 'The one thing I do...is to forget what is behind me and do my best to reach what is ahead.'"

Steve felt a new lightness enter his heart...and a greater appreciation for the unconditional love of his God.

THE SKI TRIP
by Lesley Friis

Finally, after a long, tedious fall, school broke for two weeks. Mike looked forward to spending his winter break skiing with the guys. He had saved his money for months. This would be the most fun vacation he'd ever had, just him and the guys together in a condo belonging to the family of a friend, hitting the slopes every day, coming home just in time for Christmas with his family.

Actually, coming home for Christmas was probably going to be the worst part of winter break. Too much arguing. In fact, Mike and his parents had just had a fight about the skiing trip. "We never have time with you," they said. "You barely know your little sister. Your grandparents are coming for the week

you'll be gone. Christmas is supposed to be a family time!" Guilt, guilt, guilt.

Mike responded, perhaps a little too loudly. "I've waited for months for this trip, and I am going, no matter what!" He hated the look on his parents' faces as he packed the car and left.

So all week, despite the fresh snow and Christmas lights decorating the mountain town, Mike felt guilty. He thought of his grandparents, traveling all that way to visit with 75% of his family. He wondered about his little sister's Christmas pageant at church and his failure to buy Christmas gifts for everyone before

(continued on page 2)

© Copyright 2000
Living the Good News
a division of Church Publishing Incorporated
600 Grant Street
Suite 400
Denver, CO 80203
1 (800) 824-1813

Graphic Design & Illustration:
Carolyn Klass

ATTITUDE

THIS WEEK'S TOOL (FOR COPING WITH GUILT)

Create for yourself another "tool" to help you cope with your feelings this week. Let this tool deal with feelings of guilt. Here's how:

1 Cut a tool out of construction paper—a hammer, screwdriver, saw, whatever. Try to choose a tool other than those you chose in the last two sessions.

2 Choose a Bible verse or phrase to help you cope with guilt. You could, for example, choose something from today's reading from 1 John 1, like verse 9:

"But if we confess our sins to God, he will keep his promise and do what is right: he will forgive us our sins and purify us from all our wrongdoing."

Or try this verse, 1 John 3:20:

"If our conscience condemns us, we know that God is greater than our conscience and that he knows everything."

Or use a verse you find yourself!

3 Write your chosen verse on your construction-paper tool.

4 Use the tool throughout the week whenever you're feeling guilty. Listen to God's message of forgiveness for you in the words of scripture.

Or choose something from one of these psalms, all of which deal with forgiveness:

Psalm 32:1-5
Psalm 103:1-14
Psalm 130:1-4

THE SKI TRIP *(continued from page 1)*

he left. Guilt, guilt, guilt. Mike returned to town on Christmas Eve just in time for dinner and their family gift exchange. And of course, what did his grandparents give him? A pair of expensive skis. Mike lost it. "I'm sorry. I'm sorry. I wish I'd never gone."

"It's okay, Mike. We love you and are glad you're back. Next year maybe we can spend Christmas together."

But wait a minute…

- What do *you* think about Mike's feelings of guilt? Was Mike experiencing true guilt (for doing something wrong) or false guilt (brought on by unreasonable expectations)? Was Mike being selfish or taking a well-deserved break?

- Had Mike and his parents been talking about his trip throughout the fall, what other options might they have come up with?

- In the future, how could Mike honor both his family and his desire to spend time with friends?

THE INSIDE STORY

1 JOHN 1:5-10

We're taught to feel guilty if we tell family secrets. We're taught to feel guilty if we have been abused. We're taught to feel guilty if we're not like everyone else.

This is called false guilt, that is, guilty feelings about things for which we are not responsible. False guilt is a burden that is usually imposed on us by others. It doesn't require repentance and forgiveness; it needs healing and freedom.

On the other hand, maybe we feel very little guilt about impulse spending, buying things we don't need to indulge a whim. Perhaps we don't feel guilty about putting someone down. It could be that we don't feel guilty if we sneak a peek at someone else's test.

These things deserve true guilt, that is, an acknowledgment of their wrongness and a recognition of the need to change. True guilt doesn't need to be felt; it needs to be owned. True guilt is a God-given calling to repentance.

In his epistle, John gives a simple principle to determine true versus false guilt. Does your behavior intensify your fellowship with God? If it does, then no matter what you feel (or what someone tells you that you should feel), you are not guilty. If your behavior breaks that fellowship, then you are guilty of sin.

But don't stop there. Oh, no, don't stop with the guilt. Go on to the next step. Agree with God about your guilt (that's confession), accept God's sure and complete forgiveness and demonstrate your renewed fellowship with God by stopping the behavior that got you into the guilt-pickle in the first place.

Don't be surprised at guilt. God isn't. Just use it to turn you back to God.

True guilt is a God-given calling to repentance.

LEADER'S GUIDE

FOCUS

Emotions: Joy

SCRIPTURE

John 2:1-11

SCAN

Today's meeting invites group members to celebrate their faith:
- In Attitude Check, group members practice joyfulness as they play several off-the-wall games.
- Today's Attitude Question discussion explores the nature of Christian joy, celebration, play and laughter.
- In Attitude Search, members learn that Jesus' first recorded miracle helped keep a party going.
- In Attitude Adjustment, small groups plan a closing celebration.
- Attitude Exit celebrates God's love and faithfulness.

STUFF

Bibles
photocopies of today's paper (pp. 21-22), 1 per group member
blindfold
pillow
chalkboard and chalk or newsprint and marker
colored construction paper
colored felt markers
scissors

1. Attitude Check: CRAZY JOY

Welcome group members and invite them to play any or all of the following games:

- *Hug Tag*—Hug Tag plays like an ordinary game of tag, but the "safety zones" are provided by hugs. When *It* approaches you to tag you, you can run, or you can grab someone for a 3-second hug; during the hug you're safe and can't be tagged. *It* can't stand around waiting for you but must move on to someone else.

- *Ducky Wucky*—In Ducky Wucky, players sit in a circle of chairs around a person chosen to be *It*. *It* is then blindfolded. After *It* is blindfolded, group members switch seats. *It* moves from the center of the circle and sits on a pillow on someone's lap. *It* says, "Ducky Wucky." The person upon whose lap *It* sits answers, "Ducky Wucky," disguising his or her voice to keep *It* from recognizing him or her. *It* gets two attempts to guess the identity of the person upon whose lap *It* is sitting. If *It* guesses correctly, *It* takes the place of the person guessed, and the person guessed is the new *It* in the center of the circle. After the new *It* is blindfolded, group members again switch seats and a new round begins.

- *Blob Tag*—Chose an *It*. As all group members move around the room, *It* tags one other person; *It* and the person tagged form a *Blob* by holding hands and moving together, trying to tag others. As others are tagged, they join with *It* and those already tagged, enlarging the *Blob*. The *Blob* may divide into smaller *Blobs*, as long as there are always two or more players in each *Blob*. *Blobs* can rejoin at any time. Play until all group members are part of one big *Blob*.

2. Attitude Question: WHAT IS JOY?

Discuss:
- How did you feel as you played these games? What made them fun?
- Why is playing games like this important? What good do they do?

● What different kinds of joy are there?
● How much joy do we see in our families? our church? our youth group? our school?

3. Attitude Search: JOHN 2:1-11

Distribute Bibles and recruit four volunteers to read John 2:1-11 dramatically. Assign the parts of the *narrator, Jesus' mother, Jesus* and the *man in charge of the feast.* After the reading, discuss:
● This is Jesus' first recorded miracle.
   — What event is Jesus attending?
   — How does he save the party?
   — What difference does this miracle make to the partygoers? to Jesus' followers?
● What does this story suggest about Jesus' attitude toward celebrations and having fun?

Ask group members to pair off. Say:
● With your partner, rewrite this gospel story, giving it a contemporary setting.
● Place yourselves in the story.
● What happens in your new version of the story? What part do you and your partner play? What part does Jesus play? How does Jesus help keep the celebration going? Let your story say something about the importance of joy.

Give partners time to talk over their new versions of today's story from John 2, then ask volunteers to share their stories with the group. Ask:
● What new insights have we gained today about the importance of joy in the Christian life?

4. Attitude Adjustment: PREPARING JOY

Distribute copies of today's ATTITUDE paper and invite group members individually to complete the activity This Week's Tool, printed in the papers.

When group members have finished, re-gather and continue:
● Today's meeting ends with a celebration of joy.
● First, let's decide what to celebrate: *(Ask a volunteer to list group members' answers to the following on chalkboard or newsprint.)*
   — What do you like most about God?
   — What's the best thing about being a Christian?
   — What is the greatest thing God has done for you?

When a list of 20-30 items has been compiled, continue:
● Let's plan our closing celebration. What different elements could it include? *(Ask the volunteer to also list these on chalkboard or newsprint. The celebration could include prayer, poetry, scripture, dance, music and song, speaking parts, making a vow or promise, praising, etc.)*

Let group members divide into groups depending on which element of the closing celebration they'd like to plan. Give groups 10 minutes to plan and practice their portions of the celebration.

Regather and decide the order of the elements for the celebration. Write the order on chalkboard or newsprint.

Be certain to allow a place within the celebration for volunteers to share today's construction-paper tools.

5. Attitude Exit: REJOICE!

Let group members lead and participate in the closing celebration.

a division of
Church Publishing
Incorporated

600 GRANT ST., #400
DENVER, CO 80203
1.800.824.1813

JOY

ATTITUDE
FOR TEENS BY TEENS

LIGHTEN UP! REJOICE!

by Matt Sheen

Imagine a society in which "goofing off" is strictly prohibited...

Imagine a society where it is illegal to laugh on Sunday...

Sound impossible? Had you been one of America's first settlers, these restrictions may have been a grim reality!

Many of the early Puritans and Calvinists established rigid religious laws that included public humiliation for those who, by enjoying themselves, failed to "keep the Sabbath holy."

Today we regard many of these rules as ridiculous. Instead, joyfulness plays an important role in our faith. In Paul's letter to the Philippians he says, "May you always be joyful in your union with the Lord. I say it again: rejoice!" (Philippians 4:4).

We express joy in many aspects of our faith, including praise. We worship through song, dance and music. Does God want a relationship with us that's dismal and boring? No! Our relationship with God was never

(continued on page 2)

REAL JOY
by Jessie Duvall

Many people are confused about joy. They think of joy only as an ecstatic, exhilarating emotion, and, for this reason, don't experience joy very often. While joy may be ecstatic and exhilarating, someone can also experience joy in a peaceful, solemn moment or even in times of struggle.

I like this definition: Joy is "knowing that you are in harmony with God's will." The key word is *harmony*, a beautiful sound produced when people work together. Knowing that you are in harmony with God means that you and God work together, share a common plan and live in agreement.

Using this definition, one could live a lifetime with joy. In reality, however, we all live at times out of harmony with God. We know life without joy. But how beautiful that God always invites us to return to grace and experience the harmony—the joy—once more.

So joy will not always be a "warm fuzzy" feeling. Maybe God will give us the joy of working with the poor and the outcast, the homeless or people with AIDS. Maybe we will know the joy of not getting even with someone who has made us angry. Maybe we will experience the joy of forgoing immediate pleasures like premarital sex or getting high.

We discover the deepest joy beyond the incredibly intense but brief emotion most people imagine when they think of joy. Some of the things we may pass up to stay in harmony with God become insignificant in comparison to the ultimate joy—eternal fellowship with Christ in heaven.

My prayer for you? That you always have abundant joy in your life.

© Copyright 2000
Living the Good News
a division of Church Publishing Incorporated
600 Grant Street
Suite 400
Denver, CO 80203
1 (800) 824-1813

Graphic Design & Illustration:
Carolyn Klass

ATTITUDE

Living the Good News

Create for yourself a "tool" to help you celebrate what's good about your life with God. Here's how:

1 Cut a tool out of construction paper. Pick any tool you'd like, but if you've been making tools in past sessions, pick something different now.

2 Choose a Bible verse or phrase to help you experience the joy of knowing God. You could, for example, choose something from one of the psalms, which often express joy, like Psalm 68:19:

"Praise the Lord, who carries our burdens day after day; he is the God who saves us."

Or find a verse or phrase in one of these psalms:

Psalm 66:1-9
Psalm 95:1-7
Psalm 98
Psalm 100

Or maybe this, which is Luke 10:20b:

"Be glad because your names are written in heaven."

Or this, Philippians 4:4:

"May you always be joyful in your union with the Lord. I say it again: rejoice!"

Or use a verse you find yourself!

3 Write your chosen phrase or verse on your construction-paper tool.

4 Use the tool throughout the week when you need a reminder to rejoice. Let God help you celebrate through the words of scripture.

LIGHTEN UP! REJOICE!

(continued from page 1)

meant to be a dreary task to which we resign ourselves, but something in which we take pleasure.

Our covenant with Christ fills us with security and optimism, gifts worth celebrating! Be happy in the knowledge that God is always with you. Praise God with gladness in your heart and a smile on your face.

In a word: *Rejoice!*

JOHN 2:1-11

You know, sometimes the gospel seems very solemn—all that stuff like repentance and obedience and self-sacrifice and suffering. And, of course, all these things are right and good. But if that's all we hear, we're not getting the whole picture about the gospel.

Have you been told about the joy? Christians sometimes act like it's a secret. You know, put on a glum face, look sour, make 'em think God is nothing but a cosmic Inspector checking for dirt under your nails. That's good news. That'll bring 'em into the kingdom. Yeah, right.

Take a look at Jesus. Here he is at the great transition of his life. He's spent thirty years in a carpenter's shop, a nobody in a nobody village. Now he's entering into an intense time of ministry that will lead him to the cross.

Serious stuff, wouldn't you say? But what's the first miracle Jesus performs, the first sign of his true identity? It's a party!

A party! A group of friends and family just hanging around together eating and drinking and telling old jokes and singing and dancing and celebrating. And Jesus is right there.

But it gets better. Just when it looks like the party is going to come to an early end (how happy are you when you find out the band is leaving in ten minutes and the party's just begun?), Jesus steps in and keeps the party going.

The will of God revealed in Christ Jesus included a concern for the hosts' embarrassment, sympathy for the guests of honor and a sincere interest in keeping the good times rolling.

The will of God, Jesus says, includes joy. (This said by a man whose death was part of the will of God.) Hilarious joy. Great gladness. Good news.

The will of God, Jesus says, includes joy.

LEADER'S GUIDE

FOCUS

Emotions: Jealousy

SCRIPTURE

Numbers 12:1-16

SCAN

Today's meeting invites group members to move from jealousy of others to appreciation of their own gifts and qualities:

● Attitude Check sets up a situation in which some group members may feel jealous.
● In Attitude Question, small groups share stories of jealousy and discuss jealousy's power.
● Attitude Search examines a scripture story about jealousy and its consequences.
● In Attitude Adjustment, group members uncover the relative nature of possessions, abilities and physical attributes and list suggestions for dealing with jealousy.
● Attitude Exit invites group members to affirm in themselves those qualities that might be envied by others.

STUFF

Bibles
photocopies of today's paper (pp. 25-26), 1 per group member
pens or pencils
cookies
chalkboard and chalk or newsprint and marker

1. Attitude Check: I'M JEALOUS!

Give those group members who are first to arrive at the meeting several cookies each. (Save some of the cookies to distribute later in today's Attitude Adjust-

ment.) Also give these early arrivers these instructions:

● Wait to eat your cookies until other group members have arrived. *Don't share your cookies;* you must eat them all yourselves.
● As other group members arrive—those without cookies—try to make them jealous of you and your cookies. Say things like:
  — Mmm, these are good.
  — *We* got cookies and *you* didn't! I wonder why?
  — Don't you wish *you* had gotten some cookies?

Let this continue until all group members have settled in the room and all the cookies have been eaten. Then discuss:

● What do you think is going on here?
  — Why did we give cookies to some group members and not others?
  — What were those with cookies trying to do?
● What did you think about the fact that some group members were given cookies and others weren't? How were those with cookies acting?
● How did those of you who didn't get cookies feel when you saw what was happening? How many were, to at least a small degree, jealous?
● Today's session explores jealousy. Let's move into small groups for more discussion.

2. Attitude Question: DEFINING JEALOUSY

Distribute pens or pencils and copies of today's ATTITUDE paper. Divide participants into smaller groups of 4-5 members each. Invite small groups to complete the activity Defining Jealousy, printed in the papers.

When group members have finished, regather and discuss:

● How did your group define *jealousy*?

● What were your group's best insights into jealousy?
● Let's examine a biblical example of jealousy among family members.

3. Attitude Search: NUMBERS 12:1-16

Distribute Bibles and invite group members to turn together to Numbers 12:1-16. Explain that the characters in this story—Miriam, Aaron and Moses—are siblings.

Read Numbers 12:1-16 dramatically, assigning the parts of the narrator, Miriam, Aaron and Moses. After the reading, discuss:
● Of what are Miriam and Aaron jealous?
   — When has jealousy surfaced in your family? among your friends?
● What is God's *verbal* response to Miriam and Aaron?
● What's the *physical* consequence of Miriam and Aaron's jealousy?
   — In this story, the physical consequences of jealousy are a result of God's direct intervention. How can jealousy bring its own negative consequences?
   — What has resulted from jealousy in your family? among your friends?
● In the end, Miriam is healed. How are we healed of the damage brought by jealousy?

4. Attitude Adjustment: OVERCOMING JEALOUSY

Pass out more cookies, this time giving cookies only to those group members who didn't receive any cookies at the beginning of the meeting. Invite those with cookies to try to make other members—those who received cookies earlier—jealous.

As those with cookies enjoy their snack, ask a volunteer to read aloud Nate's article, Pile O' Money, printed in today's ATTITUDE paper. Ask another volunteer to title the

chalkboard or newsprint, *From Jealousy to Appreciation*. Have this second volunteer record group members' responses to this question:
● What guidelines for dealing with jealousy can we draw from Nate's article?

Continue:
● What additional guidelines of your own can you add to our list?

Ask the volunteer to continue writing group members' ideas on the chalkboard or newsprint. Discuss:
● Which of these guidelines works best for you?
● Which of these guidelines are difficult for you?
● What role do you think God plays in helping us to overcome jealousy?

5. Attitude Exit: WHAT I'VE GOT!

Invite group members individually to complete the exercise titled Jealous of *Me?*, printed in today's ATTITUDE paper.

When members have finished, regather in a circle. Go around the circle, offering each group member a chance to affirm something about him- or herself by completing either of these statements:
● I really appreciate my...
● I really appreciate the way I...

For example, group members might say:
● I really appreciate my smile.
● I really appreciate the way I listen to others.
● I really appreciate the way I get along with my family.
● I really appreciate the way I play tennis.
● I really appreciate my self-confidence.

Encourage group members to make their statements personally affirming, a task that may be difficult for some members. Be ready to suggest the things *you* appreciate about group members; invite them to restate your suggestions for themselves.

a division of Church Publishing Incorporated

600 GRANT ST., #400
DENVER, CO 80203
1.800.824.1813

JEALOUSY

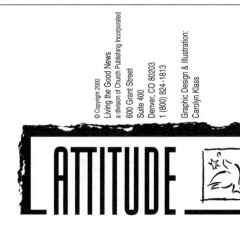

JEALOUSY by Rachel Gluckstern

i bet if franklin mason
just died i'd be the
star
of the football team

why not me?
why always them?
why can't everyone
in the world just have
the same things?
the same amount?
then no one would care
who had what

it's not fair
that should be mine
i want it
i want to look like a
model

i bet if god really
loved me
i'd be rich and
beautiful
i bet if i had a
corvette
i'd be popular

ATTITUDE
FOR TEENS BY TEENS

But, on the other hand, think of the friends of yours who have less than you. Think of what you've got that they don't.

It's all relative.

Our feelings of jealousy are based on what we have compared to what someone else has. Not too many people in America would be jealous of you for your running water, but in many other countries people would be jealous of one cup of drinkable water. We envy someone else's DVD player or big-screen TV, while someone nearby can't afford to heat their house—or can't afford the house, for that matter.

We all have more than we realize. Most of us have more than we appreciate, even if it's not huge properties and home-theater systems.

Jealousy is relative to what you have. If a person can be content with what they have, then they will not need what someone else has.

There will always be someone with more than you've got. You think you'd be happier with what they've got. But then there'd be another someone else with more than you. Where does it end?

And there will always be someone with less than you've got. They think they'd be happier with what you've got rather than what they've got. Would they?

Take a five minute break. Sit back and appreciate what you have and what you are.

It's all relative.

PILE O' MONEY by Nate Fandel

The rich Texas oil investor with the helicopter and servants walks into your office. The light reflects off of his gold teeth and gold right arm. He drops a pile o' money on the desk in front of you. The pile o' money pays for his new gold waterbed that your company has just sold him. "Thank you," he says. Even his breath smells like money. He flies off to his mansion that's bigger than a small city.

Many of us dream about what we would do if we were rich—not just rich, but so filthy rich that they'd paste our picture next to the word *rich* in the dictionary. Most of us can relate to wanting more than we have. We have friends with nicer stuff than us. The world is filled with stuff we can never afford.

© Copyright 2000
Living the Good News
a division of Church Publishing Incorporated
600 Grant Street
Suite 400
Denver, CO 80203
1 (800) 824-1813

Graphic Design & Illustration:
Carolyn Klass

ATTITUDE

Living the Good News

DEFINING JEALOUSY

With the members of your small group, work through these steps dealing with *jealousy*.

STEP 1: Define *jealousy*. Write the definition you agree on in this space:

STEP 2: Go around your small group circle, each member sharing a brief story about jealousy. Tell *real* stories, based on your own experience.

STEP 3: Discuss these questions:
- What causes jealousy? What are the roots of jealousy in our own hearts and minds?
- What are you jealous of? (Do you tend to be more jealous of material possessions? of circumstances? of jobs? of relationships? of looks? of family? of abilities?)
- Respond to this quote, from François, Duc de La Rochefoucauld, 1613–1680:
  — Jealousy contains more of self-love than of love.

JEALOUS OF *ME*?

Truth is, you've got a lot of enviable qualities. There are people out there who wish they had your...courage, humor, eyes, teeth, parents, grades, attitude...whatever!

In the space below list at least five things about yourself that you could appreciate the next time you're tempted to be jealous of someone else:

NUMBERS 12:1-16

INSIDE STORY

Let's take a poll. Everyone who likes playing second fiddle, who enjoys being overlooked, who doesn't mind others thinking you're second-rate, raise your hand. Hmmm, I don't see any hands.

I don't care who you are, you know what it feels like when someone else's qualities overshadow you. "He's gorgeous!" they say, and you're pleasant-looking. "She can do trigonometry in her sleep," they say with awe, though you, too, do well in the subject. "He's the kind of guy who makes things happen," they whisper, and you? It's that feeling of almost, but not quite; sort of, but not really; average, ordinary, commonplace. And so, inside, deep down, you wrestle with jealousy, wanting the recognition, craving the appreciation.

Well, you're normal. It's normal to want others' admiration. We all want to feel special, extraordinary, remarkable, because we *are*, each of us. If only others knew...

We can say that, from a spiritual perspective, such times are a good exercise in humility. We can also say that these experiences are frustrating, irritating, painful, unfair. It hurts to feel inferior.

Miriam knows this feeling. As a young girl, she helped save her baby brother's life by encouraging the Egyptian princess to adopt him. As an adult, she is a leader and prophet of her people. But now that baby brother, Moses, seems to be the only one who gets any credit. So she stirs up an attitude, and draws Aaron in, too.

When God confronts Miriam and Aaron, they get a clue about the best way to handle jealousy. Moses is who he is because of God; God gives to each person what God decides to give; receive what you are given, because God gives to you what God gives to no one else.

There is an old Yiddish proverb that says, "If I try to be like him, who will be like me?"

LEADER'S GUIDE

FOCUS

Emotions: Depression

SCRIPTURE

1 Kings 19:1-18

SCAN

Today's meeting explores the nature of depression and how to deal with it. *Note that the focus will be on temporary states of sadness and despondency, not clinical depression:*

- In Attitude Check, group members tell about their most depressing days.
- Attitude Question invites group members to discuss the sources of depression and how they cope with it.
- In Attitude Search, members explore Elijah's struggle with depression.
- Attitude Adjustment asks members to identify what's good and satisfying in their lives.
- In Attitude Exit, members pose each other in "human sculptures" that illustrate both depression and joy.

STUFF

Bibles
photocopies of today's paper (pp. 29-30), 1 per group member
pens or pencils
index cards, 4 per participant
chalkboard and chalk or newsprint and marker

1. Attitude Check: THE WORST DAY OF MY LIFE!

Welcome group members and distribute copies of today's ATTITUDE paper. Explain that today's meeting deals with *depression*. Invite group members to read silently the definition of depression found on page 2 of the papers. Discuss:

- Who here has felt depressed?
- What other words describe how you're feeling when you're depressed?

Invite volunteers to share stories about their most depressing days. When all who wish to share have done so, ask:

- With which stories do you identify?

2. Attitude Question: UNDERSTANDING DEPRESSION

Distribute a pen or pencil and two index cards to each group member. Explain:

- On one card, write down two or three things that can trigger depression in you. For example, losing at sports, being rejected at school or sitting home alone on a Friday night.

Allow several minutes for writing, then collect and read aloud the cards. Ask:

- Anyone here feel depressed after hearing this list?
- What triggers depression?
- On your remaining card, list two or three ways in which you typically cope with depression.

Collect and shuffle the cards. Ask a volunteer to title chalkboard or newsprint *Coping with Depression*. Read the cards aloud as the volunteer lists the items on the chalkboard or newsprint. Discuss:

- Which of these suggestions are new for you?
- Which might you try?
- Let's see how the prophet Elijah dealt with his depression.

3. Attitude Search: 1 KINGS 19:1-18

Distribute Bibles and invite group members to turn to 1 King 19:1-18.

Recruit volunteers to read verses 1-4 aloud, each volunteer reading one paragraph. Discuss:
● How is Elijah feeling?
● What reason does Elijah have to feel so down?
● When in our lives have *we* felt like everyone was after us? that we might as well be dead?

Ask volunteers to read verses 5-10 aloud, each volunteer reading one paragraph. Discuss:
● What does God do for Elijah?
● Now how does Elijah feel?
● What's happened in *our* lives when people have tried to help us out of our depression?

Ask volunteers to read verses 11-14. Discuss:
● What do you think Elijah is meant to learn from the wind, the earthquake and the fire? Already feeling like he wants to die, how do you think Elijah responds when he's nearly swept away in the wind? buried in the earthquake? burned in the fire?
● Then God speaks to Elijah in a soft whisper. What do you think God wants Elijah to understand?
● Now how does Elijah feel?

Ask a volunteer to finish the story, reading aloud verses 15-18. Discuss:
● Of what does God remind Elijah? What promises does God make about Israel's future?
● Of what do we need to be reminded when we feel depressed? How do we hear God's "whisper"?
● One thing that's clear from Elijah's story—no matter how blue he felt, no matter where he went to deal with his depression, God stuck with him, gently reminding him of the bigger picture. Let's see how we can do that in today's Attitude Adjustment.

4. Attitude Adjustment: THE BIGGER PICTURE

Distribute two more index cards to each group member. Explain:

● On one of your cards, write down two or three things that contribute to your having a really good day, a day that's satisfying, fun and fulfilling.

Allow several minutes for writing, then collect, shuffle and read the cards aloud. Discuss:
● What do these items have in common?
● What makes a day "a good day" for us?

Ask group members to list on their remaining index cards two or three ways that they can create good days for themselves.

When group members have finished writing, collect and shuffle the cards. Ask a volunteer to title another section of chalkboard or a new sheet of newsprint *Making a Bad Day Better*. Read the cards aloud as the volunteer lists the items on the chalkboard or newsprint. Discuss:
● Which of these suggestions might work for you?

5. Attitude Exit: HUMAN GUMBY®

Invite a volunteer to choose several other members to "sculpt" to illustrate depression. The volunteer poses these members in a human sculpture that communicates depression, for example, slumping the volunteers' shoulders and putting their heads down.

Ask those who have been posed to hold their positions as the group discusses what is being illustrated. After the discussion, offer prayers for people who feel blue and depressed, for example:
● God, it means so much to us to know that you're close to us, even when we feel down.

Invite another volunteer to choose and pose several more group members to illustrate joy and satisfaction. Discuss this new sculpture and close the meeting by offering prayers of joy and contentment, for example:
● Loving God, open our eyes to the good and satisfying things in our lives.

a division of
Church Publishing
Incorporated

600 GRANT ST., #400
DENVER, CO 80203
1.800.824.1813

DEPRESSION

ATTITUDE
FOR TEENS BY TEENS

WAITING FOR AN END
by Rachel Gluckstern

I'm sitting, sitting, sitting, just waiting for an end. An end to all my troubles, an end to all my sorrows, an end to my life...

I'm not sure how it all began, the emotional downward spiral that I entered. See where I've ended up? End of the line, end of the road, end of the rainbow—only there is no pot of gold.

How did it happen? Where did it begin? There was Liz, she turned away from me. I've known her for so long, but now I've been replaced by a new friend. I thought good friends didn't do that to each other.

Everything's against me now, my parents, my grades, no one cares about me. I'm alone.

Why doesn't anyone care about me? Why doesn't anyone know how lost I'm feeling? Nobody asks what's wrong. Isn't that what friends do when a friend is so obviously depressed? Not even Mark noticed—Mark who's always so perceptive. No one really cares about me; they just pretend to. All my "friends" probably laugh at me and my stupidity...

(continued on page 2)

BEYOND THE BLUES
by Jerry Berg

Moody: this word is often used to describe teenagers. Some teenagers can go through moods in a day like the national government goes through a million dollars.

People have emotional highs and lows. It's a fact, and it's normal. But when someone becomes stuck in a low mood, it can be something more serious...a major depression.

Reactive depressions usually occur in response to a loss, like the separation of parents or the death of someone close. You can still deal with life, but not as well as you usually do. You might not do as well on a test, or you don't have the energy to do physical activities.

More serious depressions don't seem linked to external causes. In severe cases they can involve delusions or hallucinations. These depressions render you unable to function at all, feeling dejected, hopeless and worthless. Thoughts and actions slow down. One psychologist described a patient this way:

"The patient appears dejected and cheerless; everything he says or does is with effort... he speaks in such a low note that one finds oneself moving close to him and speaking more loudly as if he were the one who could not hear. He says that everything is hopeless, that he is a disgrace to his family; he recalls that when he was a boy he took a paper from the newsstand and did not pay for it."*

Suicide is a concern for people in serious depression.

This isn't the kind of depression we're talking about in today's meeting, but we thought you ought to know about it, too. It requires professional treatment.

Everyone deals with changes in life. Sometimes these changes are too much for us and help is needed. What's important is that you get the help when you—or someone you care about—needs it.

*Cohen, R.A., 1975. Manic-depressive illnesses. In Freedman, A.M.; Caplan, H.I.; and Saddock, B.M., eds., *Comprehensive Textbook of Psychiatry–II,* vol. 1, pp. 1012–24. Baltimore, MD: Williams and Wilkins.

ATTITUDE

Living the Good News

DEPRESSION!

Here's the definition of *depression* we'll be using in today's meeting. Note that we're not dealing with "clinical depression," a serious illness, but rather with the occasional periods of sadness or "feeling down" that are a part of all of our lives. (To understand about more serious forms of depression, read Jerry's article Beyond the Blues.)

Depression: an uncomfortable mental state of feeling blue, dejected or discouraged, often accompanied by changes in appetite and sleep and a reduction in self-worth and energy

WAITING FOR AN END (continued from page 1)

Oh God, how can you let this happen? Don't you care? I can't live with this sad, oppressing darkness, that same darkness that has swallowed me up. Oh my God, my God, why have you forsaken me...?

My door opens and my little sister toddles in. She looks at me with her big eyes and asks me what's wrong.

"No one loves me," I say.

Her eyes grow even bigger. "No! Said no! I love you!" With that she crawls into my lap and gives me a big hug.

I love you. Three simple words, but they provide a thin life-line to grasp, a ray of light in the dark. Someone loves me, someone loves me and that's what I needed to know.

And maybe there are others.

---

1 KINGS 19:1-18

THE INSIDE STORY

This story always used to surprise me. Here's Elijah, one of God's greatest prophets, who has just come from a victory the likes of which you and I will probably never see. Out of his intimate relationship with God, Elijah has called down fire from heaven, defeated the pagan priests who opposed God and ended a three-year drought. Now he's depressed? It didn't follow.

Now I understand a little better what he was feeling, for in times of depressions, successes look like failures, opportunities look like threats and the possibilities are always bad. Hope, the fountain of life, dries up, and you're left looking at a few pennies that were thrown in in better days.

Watch Elijah. First, he feels powerlessness, fear, stress. Then he runs, leaving those close to him. Then he staggers through a desert and collapses under a broom tree, a scrappy shrub that gives a zipper's worth of shade. Finally, he prays to die.

Any of this sound familiar? Have you sought shelter under any broom trees lately?

There, in his despair, Elijah falls asleep. He is awakened by an angel's touch and the food of heaven. No answers. No promises. Just compassion and provision.

Surely we know that touch, we've eaten that food. Someone who loves us has seen our pain and touched us. Maybe that food was a pizza or a burger, but somehow it has strengthened us for the journey.

Now Elijah goes on, driven by his need to talk with God. There God listens to his complaints and speaks with gentleness. God's prescription for the blues? In the directions about kings and prophets, God reminds Elijah that all the circumstances of life are under God's control; in telling Elijah about the 7,000 faithful, God reminds him that he is not alone.

In times of depression, be still enough to hear God's "soft whisper of a voice."

LEADER'S GUIDE

FOCUS

Emotions: Anger

SCRIPTURE

Jonah 3–4

SCAN

In today's meeting, group members explore anger:

- Attitude Check introduces the topic of anger by "angering" a pre-selected volunteer.
- In Attitude Question, pairs of group members discuss their personal responses to anger.
- Attitude Search introduces Jonah, an angry figure in the Old Testament.
- In Attitude Adjustment, small groups compile options for dealing with anger.
- Attitude Exit invites group members to identify new ways to respond the next time they feel angry.

STUFF

Bibles
photocopies of today's paper (pp. 33-34), 1 per group member
pens or pencils
old, broken watch or other destroyable item "of value" (see **before the meeting** note)
block of wood
hammer
chalkboard and chalk or newsprint and marker

Before the meeting recruit a group member—whom you know to be a good actor—to play the part of an unsuspecting group member whose watch is destroyed in today's ATTITUDE CHECK. If a discarded watch isn't available, the same activity could be done, for example, using an old "prized" photo, a discarded piece of "valuable" jewelry, etc.

1. Attitude Check: SMASH IT!

Welcome group members and say:

- I need someone to volunteer an item of value, something you have with you right now.
- We will use it in our first activity.

Take the watch from the volunteer recruited **before the meeting**. Place the watch on the block of wood and smash it with the hammer. Say:

- Today's topic is *anger.*

Calmly ask the volunteer:

- How are you feeling right now?

Let the volunteer express his or her anger; for example:

- What have you done! My watch! My grandparents gave me that watch for my last birthday. Are you crazy?

Let the volunteer continue raving for a minute, then stop and explain to the group that it was a setup. Discuss:

- How convincing was our volunteer? Did you believe her (his) anger? Why or why not?
- We all handle other people's anger differently. How were you feeling when our volunteer was expressing anger?

2. Attitude Question: EXAMINING ANGER

Divide participants into pairs. Ask partners to discuss the first of the four questions printed below, allowing 2 minutes. After the 2 minutes, read the next question, again allowing 2 minutes for discussion. Continue in the same way for the remaining two questions. *Questions:*

- When do you feel angry?
- How would someone know if you were feeling angry? In other words, how do you act when you're angry?
- How do you deal your anger? What do you do to cope?

ATTITUDE FOR TEENS BY TEENS

● What have you been taught about anger? Is anger okay or not? Explain.

After the final 2 minutes, regather and discuss:
● What did you decide about that last question? Is anger okay or not? When might anger be okay? When is it not?
● In what different ways do we deal with anger? What options do we have?
● Think of people you know who are angry a lot of the time.
— What do you observe about angry people? What affect do they have on others?
— How are *you* affected by the anger of others?
— How do *you* deal with angry people?
● Let's explore the story of Jonah, an angry man from Old Testament times.

3. Attitude Search: JONAH 3–4

Distribute Bibles and invite group members to turn to the Old Testament book of Jonah.

If you are using *Today's English Version,* you will find printed in the book of Jonah an illustrated summary of the book called "Highlights from the Life of Jonah." The first two-thirds of the illustrations retell the familiar story of Jonah's attempt to flee from God, the storm at sea, Jonah being thrown overboard and finding himself left on dry land by the "large fish." Use these illustrations to summarize the first two chapters of Jonah.

If you are not using copies of *Today's English Version,* invite volunteers to summarize for the group the story of Jonah and the fish.

After this summary, read Jonah 3–4 dramatically, assigning volunteers the parts of *the narrator, the Lord, Jonah and the king of Ninevah.*

After the reading, discuss:
● Jonah gets angry twice in this story.
— Why is he angry in Jonah 4:1?
— Why is he angry in Jonah 4:9?
— When have we felt angry for similar reasons?

● What is God's response to Jonah's anger?
— Why does God think Jonah's anger is unjustified?
— What "bigger perspective" does God offer Jonah?
— When can a bigger perspective help us to deal with *our* anger?
● Let's see if we can come up with other ways to deal with anger.

4. Attitude Adjustment: HEALTHY ANGER

Distribute copies of today's ATTITUDE paper. Divide participants into smaller groups of 3-4 members each. Explain:
● You'll find directions for your small group in the activity Anger Options, printed on page 2 of your paper.
● When you've finished your discussions, we will regather and share results.

Allow 10-15 minutes for group discussion, then call participants together. Ask each group to relate:
● its chosen situation
● its two or three best options for dealing with that situation

Ask a volunteer to record the groups' options on chalkboard of newsprint. Discuss:
● What options do we have when we feel angry?
● Which options are the healthiest?
● How can we help ourselves to choose the healthier options?

5. Attitude Exit: NEXT TIME

Invite group members to stand together in a circle. Ask each group member to complete this statement:
● Next time I feel angry I will choose to...

When all who wish to complete the statement have done so, close by praying:
● Jesus, even you got angry, so we know anger isn't wrong. Help us to feel anger when it's appropriate, and to make wise choices as we express it. Help anger motivate us to make good changes in loving ways. *Amen.*

a division of
Church Publishing
Incorporated

600 GRANT ST., #400
DENVER, CO 80203
1.800.824.1813

ANGER

ATTITUDE
FOR TEENS BY TEENS

GRRR! by Jerry Berg

Your parents are fuming. Your neighbors are furious. Your siblings are ticked off.

Know the feeling? It's anger. Everyone, at one time or another, feels angry...*everyone*. And most of us think of anger as a bad thing. It's not. By itself, anger is a signal that you need to deal with something. It's how you deal with your anger that matters.

Anger can be expressed in both good and bad ways. Anger can be a positive thing. Anger can be a negative thing.

Negative ways to deal with anger include a perceived need to get re-venge. Revenge-seeking can cause serious problems, like drive-by shootings, fights and destruction of property. These are all the result of improperly vented anger. Yes, you feel angry and frustrated—you may not even know why, exactly!—but deal with the frustration rationally, not impulsively.

Positive ways of expressing anger resolve problems instead of creating bigger problems. If your anger is so great that you feel out of control, leave the situation until you calm down. Talk out your anger, first with an impartial third person, but eventually with the person at whom you feel angry. Don't scream, accuse or

(continued on page 2)

HEARING HAL by Nate Fandel

I was stepping quick to the supermarket to pick up some discount candy to give to the one-legged duck at the park, when low-and-behold a gang of ruffians jumped out of the woods and attacked me with clubs and bullwhips. They rode off into the distance with my $2.25. I knew I could never keep up with their horses, so I walked home.

Needless to say, I felt a bit angry. I was really in the mood to pummel something. It was fortunate there were no small animals around.

I had a conversation with Hal when I got home. Hal was my grandfather's beaver, stuffed by natives and traded to him for magic rocks. Actually they were gallstones. The beaver had curly sea shells for eyes.

"Hal," I said, "I am angry." Then I explained the whole story.

"Well, Nate," said Hal. "I believe patience might be the key. Think about the Jedi masters. Think about the great people of history. Do you think Abe Lincoln had much of a temper? Think about Phill the quadruple amputee, the one who lay in a ditch for a week before he was rescued. He had patience. Think about the Buddhist monks. All of these people have patience. What would Jesus advise you to do right now?"

Then Hal asked me to light his pipe. I watched the smoke rise in front of the TV. After a half hour of watching the grey static through the smoke I knew he was right. I too wanted to be cool and collected. I am a winner. I am trying to forgive them, for they know not what they do...or did.

I thanked Hal and went to sleep by the fire.

© Copyright 2000
Living the Good News
a division of Church Publishing Incorporated
600 Grant Street
Suite 400
Denver, CO 80203
1 (800) 824-1813

Graphic Design & Illustration:
Carolyn Klass

ATTITUDE

Living the Good News

ANGER OPTIONS

With the members of your small group, talk about different ways to deal with anger. Do this:

- First, have each member of your group share a recent time when he or she felt very angry. Don't tell how you dealt with the situation, just describe it.

- Second, pick one of these shared situations to talk about further.

- Third, in the space below, list the different ways that an angry person could respond in that situation. List what you think are *good* options on the left and what you think are *bad* options on the right.

Good Options	Bad Options

GRRR! *(continued from page 1)*

exaggerate, but clearly express what you are feeling, what you want and why. If you need to do something physical, take a walk, ride a bike, exercise, etc.

Above all, admit your anger, face it and deal with it. Stuffing it leads to stress and possible illness, or an

uncontrolled, dangerous blowup when the pressure gets to be too much.

Anger's a gift to alert us to the need to change something. Don't waste the gift by hurting yourself or others. Use it for good.

THE INSIDE STORY

JONAH 3–4

Jonah just can't get it right. When he first hears the word of the Lord, he tries to "get away from the Lord." Dumb idea. It gets him a reserved seat in the abdominal cavity of a fish. He changes his mind. Good idea. This gets him back to dry land.

Now he's an obedient boy. He does what God tells him to do. He marches over to nasty Nineveh and gives those pagans what's what. There. Now Jonah feels so righteous. He was good; he preached God's message. Those evil Ninevites are bad; they'll get what they deserve. So Jonah settles down in the shelter of a vine to get a good view of the destruction.

But sure enough, God, who is a loving and merciful God, always patient and always kind, decides not to punish the Ninevites. It's enough to drive Jonah crazy with rage.

Much of our anger is just like his. We feel so righteous. Instead of earning a pat on the head, we get a kick in our hindquarters. It's not fair! We've been wronged somehow and, like Jonah, we "have every right to be angry."

Yes, yes, yes. But, Jonah was missing the point, and maybe we are too. Our rights, our rewards, our claim to justice are really like the vine that "grew up in one night and disappeared the next." We care so much about what *we* want or deserve that we have failed to move into the heart of God.

There was Jonah's predicament. He had been properly obedient, but he had missed God's ultimate desire. He did what God told him to do, but he did not want what God wanted. If he had let go of his righteousness long enough to experience the compassion and kindness of God, then his anger would have dissolved like the dew before the sun.

LEADER'S GUIDE

FOCUS

Emotions: Fear

SCRIPTURE

Numbers 13:17–14:25

Scan

Today's meeting invites group members to explore what and why they fear:
- Attitude Check asks members to take part in a survey about fear.
- In Attitude Question, members discuss the nature and source of fear.
- Attitude Search examines the Old Testament story of the fearful spies.
- In Attitude Adjustment, pairs of group members face fear in a trust fall.
- Attitude Exit closes the meeting with prayers to overcome fear.

Stuff

Bibles
photocopies of today's paper (pp. 37-38), 1 per group member
pens or pencils
chalkboard and chalk or newsprint and marker

1. Attitude Check: BEING AFRAID

Distribute copies of today's ATTITUDE paper. Ask group members to take the survey titled What Do *You* Fear Most?, printed in the papers.

When group members have completed their surveys, use a spare copy of today's paper to tally the results. Poll the group for each item on the list; for each group member, score a number 1 choice 3 points, a number 2 choice 2 points and a number 3 choice 1 point.

Total points for a final score, then list on chalkboard or newsprint the group's three biggest fears. Discuss:
- What do all of the fears on the list in your papers have in common?
- What makes the three fears we picked as our biggest fears the worst?

2. Attitude Question: EXAMINING FEAR

Divide participants into smaller groups of 3-4 members each. Ask the first question listed below. Give groups 2-3 minutes to discuss the question, then call time and ask the next question. Repeat for the remaining questions. Encourage groups to give all of their members time to share after each question. *Questions:*
- What's the most afraid you've ever been?
- What types of things scare you the most? physical threats? emotional threats? social threats?
- What have you feared in the past that no longer scares you? Why has this changed?
- For the three "big fears" now listed on chalkboard or newsprint, what is the root cause of each?
- Lack of control is a big reason for fear. What part does lack of control play in the things you fear?
- How do you cope with fear? What are your options? Who helps you deal with fear?
- When is fear healthy and normal?
- When is fear unhealthy and harmful?

Distribute Bibles to group members. Ask members to remain in their small groups.

3. Attitude Search: NUMBERS 13:17–14:25

Today's reading from Numbers 13–14 is long. Divide the reading among the small groups, adjusting the size of the reading for the number of groups. For example, divide the passage as follows for 3 groups: 13:17-29, 13:30–14:10 and 14:11-25. Divide the passage as follows for 6 groups: 13:17-24, 13:25-29, 13:30-33, 14:1-10, 14:11-19 and 14:20-25. Offer groups these instructions:

● Read aloud your assigned passage.
● After the reading, plan and practice a pantomimed version of your passage to present to the other groups. Pantomiming is acting out without words.
● Through your pantomime, you'll be telling your part of the story of the spies to the other groups.

Give groups time to read, plan and practice; then invite groups, in the proper order, to present their pantomimes. Invite other groups to continuously verbalize aloud what's happening in each pantomime, much as is done in the game of Charades. Expect and allow rowdiness and good humor as pantomiming groups try to communicate the events of the story.

When all pantomimes have been presented, discuss:

● What do the spies fear?
● In your own words, what is Caleb's response to the spies' fear?
● After the spies spread their rumors, what do the people fear?
● In your own words, what is Moses and Aaron's response to the people's fear?
● What does God say is the basis of the people's fear? *(See v. 11.)*
● What's the final result of the people's fear?

4. Attitude Adjustment: FALLING PAST FEAR

Ask group members to line up according to height, from shortest to tallest. Pair group members, matching people of about the same height with each other. Explain:

● In many cases, learning to trust is a way to overcome fear, either trusting God, trusting ourselves or trusting others.
● God wanted the people of Israel to trust in God—in God's guidance and in God's protection—instead of fearing.
● Let's try some "trust falls" to illustrate getting past fear to trust.

Ask a volunteer (one about your size) to help you demonstrate a trust fall. Ask the volunteer to stand several feet in front of you, facing away from you, with arms hanging down by his or her sides. Invite the volunteer to fall backward, keeping legs and back straight and stiff. As the volunteer falls, slip your hands and arms under the volunteer's arms, catching the volunteer under the arms. Note that the riskiness of the fall can be minimized by placing the volunteer closer to you before he or she falls.

Ask pairs to practice trust falls with each other. Let them begin by having both partners stand fairly close to each other for initial catches, then slowly move apart as the *faller* comes to trust more in the *catcher*. *Assure safety when conducting this activity. Don't allow group members to take unnecessary risks.*

After several minutes of activity, discuss:

● What was easier for you, to catch or to fall? Explain.
● What fear did you experience in this activity? Explain.
● What did you experience of trust in this activity?
● What does this activity suggest to us about the other fears we face in life?
  — What does it say about the fear of failure? of rejection? of loneliness?
  — What does it say to us about the three big fears we listed in today's Attitude Question?
● How can we "fall back into the arms of God" when facing our fear?

5. Attitude Exit: FEAR PRAYERS

Stand together in a circle. Let each member pray for help with something he or she fears. Don't force anyone to pray aloud, but you might point out that one fear many of us have is the fear of praying in front of others!

Offer a closing prayer about fear:

● Jesus, what did you fear? rejection? having your friends desert you? death? Help us to rely on our friends and on God to face our fears, just as you did. *Amen.*

a division of Church Publishing Incorporated

600 GRANT ST., #400 DENVER, CO 80203 1.800.824.1813

FEAR

ATTITUDE
FOR TEENS BY TEENS

APPREHENSION MAKES IT WORSE
by Nate Fandel

Whatever I fear, it's made much worse by my worrying about it before it happens. In other words, what I fear is never as bad as I expect it to be.

I'm not talking about gut-wrenching my-life-is-in-danger fear, but about the day-to-day things, like taking tests or meeting new people. When I worry about these, it's the worry about them that's as much of the problem as the things themselves. The worry builds on itself and the problem seems to grow bigger and bigger. It's my apprehension that becomes the problem.

In addition to the apprehension beforehand, I find that lack of preparation is part of the problem, too. When I'm not in control of myself,

like when I don't know the answers because I didn't study, that's when I worry more because I'm expecting to screw up. It's the worst when I can see it coming.

Right now I'm doing fairly well. I remember to study for tests and try to know what is going on at all times in my classes. I don't like surprises when it comes to school. I take time to think through social situations in a realistic manner before they happen. This gives me the edge I need... makes me feel more comfortable. Whether that edge is real or a trick of the mind doesn't matter; what matters is that I do minimize my fear.

I like to know what's going on, and I wish I always could. But even if not, I can prepare myself as best I can.

Apprehension makes fearful situations much worse.

Being prepared for those situations makes the fear much less.

© Copyright 2000
Living the Good News
a division of Church Publishing Incorporated
600 Grant Street
Suite 400
Denver, CO 80203
1 (800) 824-1813

Graphic Design & Illustration:
Carolyn Klass

ATTITUDE

Living the Good News

4

HANDLING FEAR *by Rachel Gluckstern*

We fear many things: taking a test, losing a job, violence in our schools, meeting people, talking to people, dying, etc. Yet, when you come right down to it, there is only one thing that everyone fears: *loss*. All fears boil down to being afraid of losing something or someone.

Fear is natural and a part of life, yet it often stops us from achieving many things. It is a hindering nuisance, not a helper. Maybe we can let go of some of our fear.

Many people find help for handling fear in their belief in God. The Bible has many comforting passages

in it, telling how God is always there for us, working to overcome the things we fear.

"Even if I go through the deepest darkness, I will not be afraid, Lord, for you are with me" (Psalm 23:4a).

As a Christian, be aware that God is always with you, protecting you. Jesus Christ makes the promise that whoever believes in him will live forever.

God can't speak to you conversationally, but God does speak to you

(continued on page 2)

1

WHAT DO *YOU* FEAR MOST?

In this list of fears, circle the three things that you fear the most. Note that you can add one fear of your own at the end:

- failure
- disappointing others
- making mistakes
- feeling worthless
- serious illness
- death
- being abandoned
- the future
- loneliness

- rejection
- hell
- not being liked
- growing up
- God
- getting old
- not being in control
- violence
-

When everyone has finished their surveys, the group will gather and tally the results.

HANDLING FEAR *(continued from page 1)*

in many other ways—through other people, for example, or in your own heart. So think: How do you hear God speaking to you? And listen: What is God saying?

God loves you, but God also lets you make your own choices. You're bound to make mistakes and run into bad things along the way. Just let them pass by. Accept them and let them go, realizing that God is always with you—before, during and after the difficult times. Let God help you handle your fears.

NUMBERS 13:17–14:25

THE INSIDE STORY

The people of God are on the edge of the Promised Land. They have made it past the plagues, out of slavery, through the sea, across the desert, to the frontier. They've eaten food dropped from heaven and water flowing from a rock. Now they need only move in.

Sounds easy? Might have been. We'll never know, 'cause they listened to the craven voice of fear instead of the confident voice of God.

There on the border, Moses sent twelve men to check it out. For forty days, the men explored this land of milk and honey. They liked what they saw. It would have been a good place to settle in and raise a family. *But...* (That's fear's favorite word: *but.*)

The spies saw powerful people and fortified cities. "No, we are not strong enough to attack them...we even saw giants there....we felt as small as grasshoppers." And then, to bolster their fear (for fear always needs a lot of support), they lied about the land: "The land's no good. Couldn't make a living there. Nope, not worth the effort."

And then fear accomplished what it had set out to do. It made the horror from which the people had escaped, the bondage of Egyptian slavery, look good. "Let's go back!" Retreat! Fear always likes to make what is good look bad and what is bad look good. Otherwise we might actually be able to reach out and grasp all the goodness God wishes to give us.

And then there was Caleb. Not only was he not afraid of the Canaanites, he was not afraid to tell the truth to the Israelites: "We are strong enough."

Maybe you are on a new frontier, but the enemies look like giants and, well, maybe it isn't worth the risks. But somewhere inside you is the voice of Caleb, reaching over the thousands of years in between, saying, "The Lord is with us...so don't be afraid."

LEADER'S GUIDE

FOCUS

Love: Loving God

SCRIPTURE

Mark 12:28-30

SCAN

Today's meeting suggests that God's love for us provides the foundation for all other love:

- Attitude Check illustrates the importance of strong foundations through human pyramid-building.
- In Attitude Question, group members respond to an article describing God's love as an incredible "gift."
- In Attitude Search, group members hear Jesus' call to love God first and foremost.
- Attitude Adjustment invites small groups to present roleplays that illustrate that love involves making choices and taking action.
- In Attitude Exit, members reflect silently on God's amazing love.

STUFF

Bibles
photocopies of today's paper (pp. 40-41), 1 per group member
chalkboard and chalk or newsprint and marker

1. Attitude Check: STRONG FOUNDATIONS

Welcome participants and divide them into two teams. Invite each team to build a human pyramid, three layers tall. Expect that teams will place the largest, strongest people on the bottom of their pyramids.

Declare one team the winner, based on speed of construction and stability of the pyramid.

Repeat the activity, asking teams to build another pyramid. This time, however, instruct them to place the smallest people on the bottom of the pyramid and the biggest people on the top.

Monitor the teams' attempts to make this work, ensuring that no one risks injury. (Most groups will quickly conclude that it either can't be done or isn't worth the effort.)

Gather participants and discuss:

- Why can't we build a good pyramid putting the smallest people on the bottom?
- What does this exercise suggest about the importance of a good foundation when building a human pyramid? when preparing to do a school project? when getting ready for life?
- What other tasks in life require a solid foundation?
- On what "shaky foundations" do people build their lives today?
- What characteristics would we expect in a "sound foundation" for life?
  — How does God provide this type of foundation?
- What part does *love* play in laying a foundation for life?
  — What part does *God's love for us* play?
  — What part does *our love for God* play?

2. Attitude Question: IS LOVE THE KEY?

Divide participants into small groups of 4-5 members each. Distribute copies of today's ATTITUDE paper and invite groups to read Jessie's article Loving God, printed in the papers.

When groups have finished reading, invite them to discuss the questions printed at the end of Jessie's article.

When groups have finished discussing, ask volunteers to share their groups' most interesting responses to Jessie's article. If necessary to spark discussion, ask:
● With which of Jessie's claims do you agree? disagree? Explain.
● What was helpful in Jessie's article? Why?
● What else do you believe about God's love?
● How easy or hard is it for us to believe in God's love? to "feel" God's love?

3. Attitude Search: MARK 12:28-30

Distribute Bibles and invite group members to read in unison Mark 12:28-30. Discuss:
● How can we love God with all our *heart?* What would that look like? What actions would we see?
● How can we love God with all our *soul?* What would that look like? What actions would we see?
● How can we love God with all our *mind?* What would that look like?
● How can we love God with all our *strength?* What would that look like?
● Overall, Jesus is telling us to love God with our whole being, with everything we have and all we do.
  — How do you feel as you hear this command?
  — How can we help each other to love God in this way?
  — How can we help ourselves to love God in this way?

4. Attitude Adjustment: CHOOSING LOVE

Copy this statement on chalkboard or newsprint: *Love is not just a warm, fuzzy feeling, but a choice. More than something we feel, it is something we do.*

Ask a volunteer to read the statement aloud, then discuss:
● What does this statement mean?
● Give a practical example of the meaning of this statement from your daily life at home, at school or with friends.

Copy this statement on chalkboard or newsprint: *Our love for God begins with the realization of God's incredible love for us.*

Ask a volunteer to read this statement aloud, then discuss:
● What does this statement mean?
● Give a practical example of the meaning of this statement from your daily life at home, at school or with friends.

Ask participants to return to the small groups formed in Attitude Question. Direct groups to the activity Here's How We Love God, printed in the papers. Ask groups to complete the activity.

When groups are ready, ask them to present their roleplays. After each roleplay, ask:
● What does this roleplay suggest to us about loving God?

5. Attitude Exit: REFLECTION

Invite group members to sit quietly in a circle. Ask them to close their eyes and meditate on these words from 1 John 4, read slowly and meditatively:

This is what love is: it is not that we have loved God, but that he loved us and sent his Son to be the means by which our sins are forgiven.

Sit in silence for 1 minute before concluding the session.

a division of Church Publishing Incorporated

600 GRANT ST., #400 DENVER, CO 80203 1.800.824.1813

LOVING GOD

ATTITUDE
FOR TEENS
BY TEENS

Love builds on commitment, and the choices and actions we make to reaffirm the commitment keep the relationship going.

Such a definition of love fits for our relationship to Christ. Just like any other commitment, a commitment to Christ has to be carefully maintained in order for it to grow. A relationship with Christ requires many of the same things as a relationship with another person, including communication, trust, dedication and self-sacrifice. To have a relationship to Christ one continually makes choices and takes action.

(continued on page 2)

WHAT IS LOVE? by Matt Sheen

Mention love and what comes to mind? romantic feelings? warm, fuzzy emotions?

Love is more than an emotion or a feeling...much more.

For starters, think of love in terms of what you experience with a boyfriend or girlfriend. In a romantic relationship, we do "feel" something, but beyond the feeling lies work and dedication. Loving someone requires a conscious decision to support and care even when feelings of love may be absent. Love needs constant attention and courage to keep it strong and make it grow.

LOVING GOD by Jessie Duvall

Imagine it is your birthday. You've opened the cards with checks from Aunt Flora and Uncle Donny. Buried under the shredded wrapping paper and discarded ribbon lie new clothes from Mom and Dad and CDs from Grandma and Grandpa.

One giant present remains, wrapped in the most fabulous paper—everyone's favorite color—with a perfect bow and ribbon. No one seems to know who it is from; there is no card, and no one saw anyone deliver it. The wrapping carries no name or address.

You open this mysterious gift... and discover inside the incredible gift of eternal salvation, of life lived forever with God. And as if this gift of salvation is not enough, you discover other gifts buried in the tissue paper within the box, gifts of mercy, love, peace and grace. This gift needed no card; you know that it could only come from God.

Imagine now that it is a different time of year, the time for God's birthday. You remember the gifts that came for you on your birthday, and you yearn to give God just as great a gift.

You start at the mall. You shop and shop, finally returning home, empty-handed, frustrated. The task is not so easy. DVDs, clothes, stuffed animals, camping equipment...nothing seems quite right for God. Somewhere is the right gift, something big enough for God.

Then you think of it. The gift God really wants...is *you*.

God wants the only thing that you can give that God doesn't already have: *you*. You have the choice to give yourself to God. And giving your self and your love to God is something any one of us can do. This gift, more than any other, will give God pleasure.

When we consider the incredible gifts God gives to us, can we give God this in return?

Discuss it:

- Respond to Jessie's assertion that "God's love is an incredible gift." Do you agree or disagree? Explain.
- Respond to Jessie's assertion that "God takes great pleasure in our loving God back." Do you agree or disagree? Explain.
- Respond to Jessie's assertion that "loving God is our only possible response." Do you agree or disagree? Explain.

© Copyright 2000
Living the Good News
a division of Church Publishing Incorporated
600 Grant Street
Suite 400
Denver, CO 80203
1 (800) 824-1813

Graphic Design & Illustration:
Carolyn Klass

ATTITUDE

Living the Good News

HERE'S HOW WE LOVE GOD

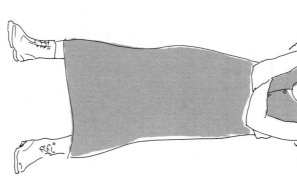

With the members of your small group, plan a roleplay illustrating one way to love God. Let your role-play demonstrate concretely an action that shows love for God.

As you plan, think broadly:

• maybe you show your love for God in something you do for others

• maybe you love God by treating your own body with respect

• maybe your love for God is shown by how you live joyfully and gratefully, using the gifts God has given you

Plan and practice your roleplay and be ready to present it to the other groups. Make sure everyone in your small group has a part.

WHAT IS LOVE? *(continued from page 1)*

Love for God and love for another person are similar, but it takes even greater faith and commitment to love someone who is not physically tangible.

To love God is, yes, to feel gratitude and warmth for God, but more importantly, to love God is to commit to following God, choosing to trust and act even when the feeling is hard to find.

THE INSIDE STORY

Let your love for God be passionate, undivided, reflective, energetic.

MARK 12:28-30

Are you a list maker? You know, the compulsive type that doesn't attempt anything without making a list? A list of things to get at the store. A list of steps in a project. A list of tasks for Saturday morning. A list of homework assignments due this week. Some of us are such chronic list makers that we put on our lists things we've already done so that we get the satisfaction of checking them off.

The religious leaders in Jesus' day were like that. They liked lists of things they were supposed to do or not do. They had big things on their lists, like not murdering, and little things on their lists, like giving God one-tenth of their seasoning herbs.

One of their favorite pastimes (kind of like arguing about who's the best player in the NBA) was rearranging their lists. They would bicker over which things were A priorities, which were B priorities, which were C, etc.

One of the religious teachers asked Jesus to pinpoint #1. "What should be the first thing on our list?" he asks.

Jesus doesn't hesitate. It's a good question, and he knows the answer. It's not an opinion. It's an answer, for them and for us. What should be #1 on all our lists?

Be a God-lover. A God-lover, Jesus says, is someone who knows that there is just one God and whose entire life (all the other things on our lists) serves one purpose: loving God.

Not a Sunday morning love. Not a five-minute-a-day love. Not a church-group-only love. Not a mental set-of-beliefs love. Let your love for God be passionate, undivided, reflective, energetic. And then all the other things on your list will fall into place.

LEADER'S GUIDE

FOCUS

Love: Loving Yourself

SCRIPTURE

1 Timothy 4:12-16

SCAN

Today's meeting proposes that a healthy love for others is built not only on our love for God but also on our love for ourselves:
- In Attitude Check, group members affirm themselves in a game of Tag.
- Attitude Question explores healthy self-regard.
- St. Paul affirms group members in today's Attitude Search.
- Group members create a chain of personal affirmations in today's Attitude Adjustment.
- In Attitude Exit, members pray for future growth while embracing God's unconditional love, right now.

STUFF

Bibles
photocopies of today's paper (pp. 45-46), 1 per group member
2" x 9" paper slips, cut from colored construction paper, 3 per group member (standard construction paper will yield 6 slips per sheet)
stapler
pens or pencils

1. Attitude Check: ME TAG

Welcome group members and invite them to play a new form of Tag, called Me Tag. Explain:

- Me Tag plays like an ordinary game of tag, but you provide your own "safety zone" by saying one positive thing about yourself.
- Each positive thing you say about yourself protects you for 3 seconds.
- Whoever is *It* may not wait for the 3 seconds to end but must move on to tag another group member.

Choose someone to be *It*. Play the game for 5-10 minutes, then discuss:
- How does it feel to blurt out something positive about yourself?
- How hard or easy was it to think of self-affirmations?
- What sort of self-affirmations were we hearing most often? Did we tend to affirm our physical abilities? mental abilities? personality characteristics?
- Why might saying positive things about ourselves be harder for some of us?

2. Attitude Question: IS LOVE THE KEY?

Distribute copies of today's paper and invite group members to read silently Jessie's article Put *Your* Mask on First.

When group members have finished reading, gather and discuss:
- Do you agree or disagree with Jessie's analogy about the airplane oxygen mask? Explain.
- Why is loving yourself important?
  — In what ways does loving yourself free you to love others?
  — Why does disliking yourself make it harder to love others?
  — What are the negative consequences of not loving yourself?
  — What are the benefits of a healthy self-love?
- Describe the difference between loving yourself (as Jesus urges us to do) and being selfish.

ATTITUDE FOR TEENS BY TEENS

3. Attitude Search: 1 TIMOTHY 4:12-16

Distribute Bibles and invite a volunteer to read aloud 1 Timothy 4:12-16 as other group members follow along. Discuss:
● When have people looked down on you because of your youth?
● Why do you think Paul urges you not to let this happen?

Divide group members into five groups. Assign each group one of the five areas mentioned by Paul in verse 12: *speech, conduct, love, faith* and *purity*. Explain:
● With the members of your small group, come up with three concrete ways to be an example in the area assigned to your group.
● Don't think only of being an example for your peers, but also for your parents, your teachers and for our church.
● Prepare to act out these ways for the larger group when we regather.

Give groups time to prepare, then invite groups to present their enactments.

4. Attitude Adjustment: AFFIRMATION CHAIN

Distribute pens or pencils and three slips of 2" x 9" construction paper to each group member. Ask group members to complete the activity I'm Great!, printed in their papers.

When group members have completed the activity, continue:
● Together we will make a paper chain of our self-affirmations.
● Choose three of your self-affirmations to copy to your slips of construction paper, one affirmation to each slip.
● Write on only one side of each slip, then fold each slip in half lengthwise to form a 1" x 9" slip.

● Loop one of your slips and staple the ends to form one link for the chain. Loop and staple a second slip through the first to form a two-link chain.
● Loop and staple your third slip through a link in someone else's chain.

Continue until all group members' slips are looped, stapled and joined into one long chain.

Note: In smaller groups, let each group member prepare four or five slips to create a longer chain.

Continue with today's Attitude Exit.

5. Attitude Exit: UNCONDITIONAL ACCEPTANCE

Stand together in a circle with as many group members as possible holding the Affirmation Chain created in Attitude Adjustment. Explain:
● In a moment you'll be asked to share two things:
 — First, tell us something you like about yourself.
 — Second, share with us something you would like God to help you change about yourself.
● After each person has shared, the rest of us will respond in unison with this response:
 — God loves you as you are. God invites you to grow.

Lead the group in this closing litany. Make it clear that, though the opportunity to speak moves from person to person around the group, individuals may pass if they choose to.

When the chain is done, tape or tack it to a wall or the ceiling of your meeting space as a reminder of God's invitation to us to love ourselves.

a division of
Church Publishing
Incorporated

600 Grant St., #400
Denver, CO 80203
1.800.824.1813

LOVING YOURSELF

ATTITUDE
BY TEENS FOR TEENS

PUT *YOUR* MASK ON FIRST by Jessie Duvall

If you've ever flown in an airplane, you know the routine. Before the plane leaves the ground, the flight attendants explain the safety procedures. They point out that your emergency exits, explain that your seat cushion doubles as a flotation device, and then say something like:

In the event of a loss of cabin pressure, oxygen masks will drop from the overhead compartments. Please place the mask over your face, pulling on the straps to tighten. *If you are traveling with small children, please put your mask on first before assisting the child.*

What kind of selfish parent, I wondered, would put her own mask on before helping her child? Isn't

the child unable to help himself? Doesn't he depend on his parent for everything?

Then someone explained it to me: If a parent insisted on putting the child's mask on before her own, she puts both their lives at risk. Without a mask, the parent might run out of oxygen and be unable to do whatever else may be required to save the child. But by taking care of herself first, the parent makes it possible to take care of the child as well.

This oxygen-mask analogy fits for lots of things in life, but it is especially true when talking about loving oneself. Many people believe that to meet your own needs before

(continued on page 2)

HEALTHY SELF-LOVE by Lesley Friis

"Love yourself."

Sound selfish?

It isn't. Love for yourself is a part of healthy self-confidence. Even the Bible mentions it: "Love your neighbor as you love yourself" (Matthew 22:39b).

So let's think about this. We agree that we must love our neighbors, right? But how? By loving ourselves. It is really very simple: before we love others we must have a healthy love for ourselves. God planned it that way.

When I think about people having healthy self-love, I think of my youth leaders Dana and Carla. Each

week they spend four hours with young—and sometimes obnoxious—teenagers. I sometimes wonder how they do it. They do it with faith, coupled with a healthy love for themselves. They have enough respect for and confidence in themselves to know that God can use them (and wants to use them) to love others to Jesus. Knowing and accepting themselves, they have the capacity to know and accept us.

Dana and Carla know their faults. They know their need for God. They know they stand forgiven before God. They love their forgiven selves just as God does, warmly, totally, unconditionally.

And so they embrace each of us, not demanding impossible standards, not expecting perfection, just opening their arms and hearts to receive us the way God has received them.

Love yourself. If God loves you, why would you do any less?

© Copyright 2000
Living the Good News
a division of Church Publishing Incorporated
600 Grant Street
Suite 400
Denver, CO 80203
1 (800) 824-1813

Graphic Design & Illustration:
Carolyn Klass

ATTITUDE

Living the Good News

I'M GREAT!

Yes, God wants you to affirm yourself. God celebrates you. God delights in you. God wants you to feel as good about yourself as God feels about you.

What can you affirm about yourself? Fill in each box with a separate self-affirmation. Here are some examples to help you get started:

- The way I make others laugh is terrific.
- My ability to listen to people when they're hurting is a great gift.
- I appreciate my ability to get things done right away without procrastinating.

So go ahead; *affirm yourself!*

PUT *YOUR* MASK ON FIRST *(continued from page 1)*

another's needs is a mark of selfishness, much like I viewed a parent putting on her own oxygen mask before helping her child. Unless we tend to our own basic needs first, however, we will be like the parent uselessly struggling to give her child oxygen without first putting on her own mask.

We need to recognize the times when we lack "oxygen," that is, self-love. We might think we're helping someone else, but we may in fact be getting in the way, putting both the other person and ourselves at greater risk.

Don't be afraid to stop and put your own "oxygen mask" on first.

Your mask may come in the form of quiet contemplation, talking with God or making a list of qualities that you possess and are proud of. Whatever your oxygen mask looks like, please remember to use it when you feel like all the air's been sucked from your life. You need to first receive your own love before you can effectively release it to anyone else.

And once the person on the plane has her mask on, though it may have taken a little extra time to put it on before helping others, she now has the ability to help the whole airplane. So too will we have the ability to reach anyone if we only love ourselves first!

---

1 TIMOTHY 4:12-16

THE [ ] INSIDE STORY

It's not easy loving yourself.

How would you finish this sentence: *If only I were...?*

Most people feel uncomfortable with themselves in one way or another. How can we help it when the whole world is telling us about others who have achieved so much, who look so beautiful, who are so smart or rich or talented?

The people around us are watching to see how we compare. We're busy watching them watching us, and it's hard to measure up to those expectations. If only...

It's not easy loving yourself, appreciating your uniqueness, being comfortable with who you are and who you aren't. It's risky business because it means throwing the opinions of other people out the window, sitting down with yourself and embracing the gifts God has given you.

Timothy struggled with this. He might have finished the sentence this way: *If only I were older and more experienced, then people would respect me.*

Paul says, in effect, "Timothy, hang it up. You're young, yes, but don't let that keep you from doing and being all that God has planned for you. In fact, you can be an example for others when you focus instead on your life of faith."

Don't watch other people to find out how valuable you are. "Watch yourself," Paul says, and you will find a rich place of opportunity and gifting and love.

LEADER'S GUIDE

FOCUS

Love: Loving Your Enemies

SCRIPTURE

Matthew 5:43-48

SCAN

In today's meeting, group members propose practical ways to love our enemies:

● Attitude Check introduces the topic of enemies in a game of Hand-Shake Killer.
● In Attitude Question, group members define enemies and discuss what Jesus may have meant when he tells us to love them.
● In Attitude Search, group members rewrite Jesus' familiar command to love our enemies.
● In Attitude Adjustment, members work through a possible process to help in loving those they find difficult to love.
● Attitude Exit offers members an opportunity to pray for people they find unlovable.

STUFF

Bibles
photocopies of today's paper (pp. 49-50), 1 per group member
deck of playing cards
pens or pencils
chalkboard and chalk or newsprint and marker

1. Attitude Check: HAND-SHAKE KILLER

Welcome group members and invite them to play a game of Hand-Shake Killer. Explain:

● In this game, one person in the room will be selected as the *killer*. The *killer* tries to eliminate as many other play-

ers as possible before being discovered.
● As we play, we all move about the room shaking hands with each other.
● *The killer* strikes by scratching the palm of another player's hand with one finger as they shake hands.
● If the person whose hand you shake scratches your palm, you're "dead"! But count to 10 slowly before you "die." The more dramatically you "die," the better!
● All *victims* are out of the game and must remain silent.
● The rest of us will try to guess the identity of the *killer* before being "killed" ourselves. But be careful: a false accusation means you're "dead" too!

From the deck of cards select as many cards as there are players in the game. Make sure one of the cards is the Ace of Spades. Shuffle the cards and distribute to players. The player who receives the Ace of Spades is the *killer*.

Play several rounds of the game, giving other volunteers a chance to play the *killer*. Then discuss:

● What cues helped us figure out who the *killer* was?
● The *killer* comes disguised as a friend, shaking hands. When in life do our "enemies" sometimes disguise themselves as "friends"?

2. Attitude Question: WHO ARE MY ENEMIES?

Write the word *enemy* in large letters at the top of chalkboard or newsprint. Ask a volunteer to record group members' answers to this question:

● What's an enemy?

After a variety of answers have been recorded on chalkboard or newsprint, continue the discussion:

- In Matthew 5:43-44, Jesus says, "You have heard that it was said, 'Love your friends, hate your enemies.' But now I tell you: love your enemies and pray for those who persecute you..."
  - What do you think Jesus means by *enemy* in these verses?
  - Why do you think Jesus wants us to love our enemies?
- What does it mean to love an enemy? What will that love look like? feel like?

3. Attitude Search: MATTHEW 5:43-48

Distribute Bibles and invite group members to turn together to Matthew 5:43-48. Ask volunteers to read this passage aloud, each volunteer reading one verse.

After the reading, title chalkboard or newsprint *Matthew 5:43-48, OGV (Our Group Version)*. Invite group members to orally rewrite these verses from Matthew 5, one verse at a time.

As you settle on a new way to state each verse, write it beneath the title on chalkboard or newsprint. For example, verse 43 could be rewritten:
- All along I've thought, "I'll be nice to people who are nice to me, and ignore the people who aren't nice to me."

Continue for all verses, encouraging group members to use contemporary language and to speak from their own experience.

When all six verses have been rewritten, read the new version in unison and discuss:
- What new insight into loving our enemies do we gain from our rewrite of Matthew 5:43-48?

4. Attitude Adjustment: LEARNING LOVE

Distribute pens or pencils and copies of today's ATTITUDE paper. Invite individuals to complete the activity Learning to Love.

When group members have finished, re-gather and invite volunteers to share the process with the group. Ask volunteers to keep to themselves the actual names they've written.

Discuss:
- How helpful is this process?
- What other ways of coping with difficult people (learning to love enemies) can you suggest?
- Today's Attitude Exit suggests another way to follow Jesus' command.

5. Attitude Exit: PRAYING FOR ENEMIES

Offer group members an opportunity to pray for their enemies. Explain:
- It's hard to sustain bad feelings for someone when you're intentionally wishing them good.
- Praying for our enemies is a loving action that can help us get beyond our feelings of anger or resentment.
- In today's closing prayer, pray for someone you have trouble loving; pray for them what you would pray for yourself.
- Don't name the person in your prayer; God will know who you mean.

Begin the prayer by offering a prayer such as:
- God, I pray for this person at work who acts like I don't count. I pray that you will give her a good week and help her do well at her job.

a division of Church Publishing Incorporated

600 GRANT ST., #400
DENVER, CO 80203
1.800.824.1813

LOVING YOUR ENEMIES

ATTITUDE
FOR TEENS BY TEENS

CARL by Lesley Friis

Carl is a nerd. Nobody likes him.

Carl loves school. He maintains a 4.0, gets involved in every school activity and—worst of all—is the teacher's pet...in every, single class. This teacher's pet business is the killer. I mean, who likes a kid whom teachers drool over, always calling on him to answer the questions, always praising him for his accomplishments? Bleah!

Carl brags, too. He gladly tells anyone within earshot about his grades, his honors, all the stuff he has done and is doing and will do.

Truth is, Carl feels desperate to be liked. He hopes people will like him because he works so hard. He keeps thinking that if he says it all loud enough and often enough, people will notice and look up to him, maybe even like him.

One Thursday, life is particularly hard on Carl. He walks home despondently. Earlier, a group of classmates threatened to beat him up for making them look bad in front of the teacher. Clearly, plainly, they had said, "Carl, nobody likes you. Stay out of our lives. We hate you." And for the first time, Carl hears them.

And as he walks, broken, Carl mutters to himself, "You don't hate me half as much as I hate you. You are my enemies, and I will find a way to get even. I no longer want you to like me, but I will make certain that you fear me."

(continued on page 2)

HARD LOVE by Matt Skeen

Quick, who are your "loved ones"?

Images of family members and close friends come to mind, right? You think of brothers and sisters and parents, sweethearts and school friends and the family pet.

I bet you didn't think of bullies, criminals and income-tax agents.

We think of those we are to love as the people who are closest to us and who wish us well. Yet Jesus tells us that loving these people is easy. Of course we love them! Who wouldn't? The tough part is loving those who wish us harm or ill will. Yet that's what Jesus expects of us; "Love your enemies," he says.

For many Christians it's hard to know how to act with people who treat us rudely or with outright dislike. How do we love our enemies? Here are some tips:

- Realize that loving someone doesn't mean feeling good about them, it means choosing to do what's best for them. We can always make that choice, even if we don't "like" them.

- Ask for God's help. God wants you to love your enemies, so take advantage of God's resources to do it. Try praying something like, "God, she drives me crazy, but I know you want me to do what's best for her. Please show me how."

- Think about how you would like to be treated, even by those who disagree with what you believe or how you live. Treat others in this way.

- Recognize that loving your enemies (doing what's best for them) will probably change the way you feel about them, making loving them even easier. Loving your enemies puts your heart at rest, and that's a great benefit. Hating someone tears you up inside. Choose to let it go.

- If you're losing control when facing an "enemy," take time out. Talk it over with someone else, then return to the situation when you've calmed down. And always remember, no matter what someone else thinks of you, God loves you and is with you.

© Copyright 2000
Living the Good News
a division of Church Publishing Incorporated
600 Grant Street
Suite 400
Denver, CO 80203
1 (800) 824-1813

Graphic Design & Illustration:
Carolyn Klass

ATTITUDE
Living the Good News

LEARNING TO LOVE

1 Pick someone you have trouble loving.

Example: A.J.

Write that person's initials here: _____

2 Identify why this person is tough to love. Think in terms of *behaviors*. What things does this person *do* and *not do* that you *do not* like?

Example: A.J. is critical of everyone, always cutting people down and making fun of them.

Describe those behaviors/actions here: _____

3 Now think *behind* the behaviors, to the person who acts in ways you don't like. What about the person might lead him or her to do these things?

Example: Ask, "Why does A.J. always cut people down?" Maybe it's her way of feeling okay about herself, because other people might be worse.

Write your theory about the "why" behind the behavior here: _____

4 Now, looking at the person behind the behavior (and not the behavior), what could you do to help that person no longer need the behavior?

Example: Maybe befriending A.J. will help her feel better about herself.

Write your ideas here: _____

CARL (continued from page 1)

And that's the end of the story... which you may not like, since you probably want something more to happen.

But you can complete Carl's story. Jesus says, "Love your enemies." So think about this:

- In the first part of the story, who are the enemies? Is Carl an enemy? Carl's teachers? the other students? What makes an "enemy"? How could the students in the story have better loved their

- "enemy" Carl? How could Carl have better loved the other students? How could Carl have better loved himself?

- It's possible that Carl's greatest "enemy" is not other students but his own pride. How can Carl love this "enemy"?

- What "Carls" do you know in your life? In what sense are they your "enemies"? How might Jesus be asking you to love them?

MATTHEW 5:43-48

THE [ ]

Jesus gets right to the heart of the gospel in these few verses. First he quotes a popular slogan, then he turns our world upside down.

"Love your friends, hate your enemies." That was the old motto. Sounds reasonable. Loving our friends comes naturally, and what else are enemies for but to hate?

Think about your enemies for a minute. They are the ones you don't speak to and who don't speak to you. They're the ones who drive you crazy with their weird habits. They're the ones who sneer at your interests or values. They're the ones you hope don't call. They're the ones who use you and dump you. You know who they are.

Jesus says that you must love them, pray for them, speak to them. As far as it is possible with you, you must be in a relationship of peace with them.

ARRGH! No way!

But Jesus points out that this is what God is like, embracing and caring for those who reject everything about God. God's goodness spreads over those who deserve it and those who don't.

In the same way, our loving spirit must welcome those who agree with us and those who don't, those who act like we do and those who don't, those who like us and those who don't, those who love us and those who hate us.

Unreasonable? Perhaps. Difficult? Definitely. Rewarding? Ask Jesus.

INSIDE STORY

God's goodness spreads over those who deserve it and those who don't.

LEADER'S GUIDE

FOCUS

Love: Loving Your Neighbor

SCRIPTURE

Luke 10:25-37

SCAN

In today's meeting, group members respond to God's call to love others:

- In Attitude Check, group members play Darling, If You Love Me, thus introducing today's topic, "loving neighbors."
- Attitude Question examines and compares the different "calls to love": loving God, loving yourself, loving your enemies and loving your neighbor.
- In Attitude Search, Jesus defines "my neighbor" in the parable of the helpful Samaritan.
- In Attitude Adjustment, small groups compose acrostic poems about loving others.
- Attitude Exit invites members to verbalize ways in which they see Christ in each other.

STUFF

Bibles
photocopies of today's paper (pp. 53-54), 1 per group member
newsprint or poster board, 1 sheet for every 3-5 group members
colored felt markers

1. Attitude Check: DARLING, IF YOU LOVE ME

Welcome group members and ask them to sit in chairs in a circle. Invite them to play Darling, If You Love Me. Choose one person to be *It* and explain:

- *It* stands in the middle of our circle.
- *Its* goal is to get any one person in the circle to laugh.
- *It* approaches someone in the circle and says to them, "Darling, if you love me, let me see you smile."
- The person approached must answer, without laughing, "Darling, I love you, but I just can't smile."
- *It* may repeat the request two more times (for a total of three times) before moving on to someone else in the circle.
- If *It* gets someone to smile, that person becomes the new *It* in the center of the circle. The old *It* takes the new *Its* place in the circle.

Encourage group members to ham it up as they play, using different voices and movement to invoke smiles. *No tickling allowed.*

After playing for a while, discuss:

- Over the last few weeks we've explored different aspects of love.
- What have we discovered about loving God?
- What have we discovered about loving ourselves?
- What have we discovered about loving our enemies?
- In today's meeting, we'll hear God ask us to love each other.

2. Attitude Question: WHO'S MY NEIGHBOR?

Distribute copies of today's ATTITUDE paper. Divide participants into small groups of three to five members each. Ask groups to complete the activity Who's My Neighbor, printed in the papers.

When groups have finished their discussions, regather participants and invite representatives from each group to share their group's best insights.

ATTITUDE FOR TEENS BY TEENS

Invite group members to discover more about loving others in today's Attitude Search.

3. Attitude Search: LUKE 10:25-37

Distribute Bibles and recruit three volunteers to read Luke 10:25-37 dramatically. Assign the parts of *the teacher of the law, Jesus* and *the narrator.*

In addition, recruit seven other volunteers to pantomime the people in Jesus' parable in verses 30-35, including *the traveler, the two robbers, the priest, the Levite, the Samaritan* and *the innkeeper.*

Ask the first three volunteers to read the story. Invite the remaining volunteers to pantomime the parable as the person reading the part of *Jesus* reads verses 30-35.

After the reading and pantomime, discuss:
● How did the Jews of Jesus' day feel about priests and Levites? (*They were highly respected.*)
● How did the Jews of Jesus' day feel about Samaritans? (*They were disliked and shunned.*)
● Jesus tells his story to Jewish listeners. Why would he choose a Samaritan to be the "neighbor" in his story? What would that say to Jesus' listeners?
● Think of someone today who is a "Samaritan" to you, someone whom you dislike and tend to shun. What would it take for you to let your "Samaritan" be a neighbor to you?
● In verse 37, Jesus tells the teacher to do what the Samaritan did, to be good to those people who rejected and shunned him.
   — Who do you know who rejects and shuns you?
   — How can you be a neighbor to this person?

4. Attitude Adjustment: POETRY OF LOVE

Ask participants to return to the small groups of Attitude Question. Distribute a sheet of newsprint or poster board and several felt markers to each group. Explain:
● Down the left side of your newsprint (poster board), write in large, capital letters the words LOVING OTHERS.
● Write an acrostic poem, using the letters of Loving Others as the first letters of each line in the poem.
● For example:
   Love looks like this:
   Offering to help
   Viewing through others' eyes
   Imagining the best...
   etc.

Ask groups to gather and read their poems for the other groups. Discuss:
● What do all our poems have in common?
● What do we learn about loving others from our poems?

5. Attitude Exit: SEEING CHRIST'S LOVE

Stand in a circle. Ask each member of the group to turn to the person on his or her left and complete the statement:
● One way in which I see Christ's love in you is...

After all group members have offered an affirmation—and been affirmed—say:
● Hug four people before you leave!

a division of Church Publishing Incorporated

600 Grant St., #400
Denver, CO 80203
1.800.824.1813

LOVING YOUR NEIGHBOR

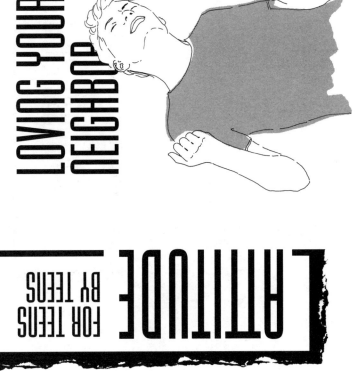

ATTITUDE

BY TEENS FOR TEENS

LAST CHANCE by Rachel Gluckstern

Ryan slammed his locker shut and pulled on his motorcycle jacket.

"Hey, Turner!" someone shouted.

Ryan looked up.

The voice continued, "Yeah, you, punkboy! Just so you know, Slate's going to kick your butt the second you walk out of school! He didn't like you defending your pretty friend Rob."

Ryan yawned. "You tell Slate I'm going to pound him into the pavement...that is, if he ever gets up the nerve to face me."

Meg, Ryan's girlfriend (and best friend of seven years) stepped around the corner. "What do you think you're doing?" she asked him.

"Danny Slate was talking trash about Rob. You think I'll let him get away with that? No way. He's toast."

When it came to his friends, Ryan Turner was the best you could want. And he was the worst enemy you could have. His fierce loyalty had gotten him into numerous scrapes.

(continued on page 2)

LOVE YOUR NEIGHBORS

by Matt Skeen

How can I love the ones next door
When they seem rotten to the core?

Jesus says, "Love humankind,"
And so I'll put dislike behind,
And try and try with all my might,
To spread the word and do what's right.

Not everyone is hard to like,
There's Tom and Sara, June and Mike—
All my friends from church and school—
I like to think are pretty cool.

But I will follow Christ's command
And love the people I just can't stand,
As if they were my brother dear.
For with the Lord I need not fear.

The evil I see throughout the land
Will be redeemed by God's just hand.

ATTITUDE

Living the Good News

WHO'S MY NEIGHBOR?

When Jesus was asked about the most important commandments, he said, "Love God. Love your neighbor as you love yourself" (Mark 12:30-31).

With the members of your small group, discuss the following questions. Be ready to share your group's best insights when we regather:

- How is "loving others" different from loving God? How is it the same?

- Who is easiest to love in your life? What makes them easy to love? How do you show your love for them?

- Why do you think Jesus puts so much emphasis on loving others? Why is it important?

- Who loves you the best? How do you know they love you? How do they show that love to you? Who do you love in this same way?

LAST CHANCE (*continued from page 1*)

"Ryan, you know what will happen if your parole officer finds out you've been in another fight. Slate's got a knife; it'll get rough."

Ryan shrugged. "No one's going to find out, so there's no danger."

Meg groaned. "They *will* find out. Then you'll be hauled off to wherever." She paused. "And then what will happen to your mother?"

"That was a low shot, Meg." Ryan was devoted to his mother. He was her main support. If he were taken away, she wouldn't be able to survive on her own, and Ryan knew it.

Seeing she was getting somewhere, Meg added, "Ryan, I'd miss you too. Can't you walk away for me?"

Ryan looked at her. She was the greatest. He'd do anything for her.

He put his arm around her. "I've decided to go home a different route." They headed down the hall. "Love," he said, "confuses the heck out of me."

Think about it:

- Who loved whom in this story? For example, in what ways did Meg love Ryan? Ryan love Meg? Meg and Ryan love Slate?

- When does loving others mean making hard choices?

- Where can we turn for the resources to love others?

THE INSIDE STORY

How much do I have to love? How far does it have to go?

LUKE 10:25-37

Jesus usually says more than people want to hear. Ask a simple question, *get a spiritual jolt?* It's a dangerous thing, asking questions of Jesus.

"Teacher," the man asks, "what must I do to receive eternal life?" At first it looks like a plain answer. Jesus and the man agree that eternal life is a result of loving God and loving your neighbor.

"Well," the man continues, "I know who God is...but who is my neighbor?" The unspoken question is: Who is entitled to my love? Who qualifies? my family? the people next door? my co-workers? How much do I have to love? How far does it have to go?

Then Jesus lets him have it. Much, much more than he wants to hear. Jesus tells him a story where the good guys become the scoundrels, and the local dirt ball becomes the hero. The men, concerned with their own agenda, their own safety, their own spirituality (the priest and the Levite) fail the test. The Samaritan (the despised foreigner), who acts on the basis of the need he sees, not on the basis of his own interests, becomes the model for neighbor-love.

If we are caught up with just exactly what we must do to qualify for eternal life, if we care only about the absolute minimum demands of love, we will never discover our neighbor.

Your neighbors are the ones in your face. Unless you're too busy keeping all the rules, you can't miss 'em.

LEADER'S GUIDE

FOCUS

Transitions: Divorce

SCRIPTURE

Psalm 27

SCAN

Today's meeting explores *divorce*, a transitional event that brings great change to teenagers' lives:

- In Attitude Check, group members identify the problems and hurts that can lead to divorce.
- Attitude Question invites members to share their firsthand knowledge of divorce.
- In Attitude Search, members find assurance that God—unlike earthly friends and family members—never deserts them.
- Attitude Adjustment uses newspaper "houses" to illustrate the flimsiness of a marriage not founded on God.
- Attitude Exit uses blocks or bricks to illustrate the relative sturdiness of a marriage founded on God.

STUFF

Bibles
photocopies of today's paper 8 (pp. 57-58), 1 per participant
rocks, about the size of eggs, 1 per participant
black, permanent markers
old newspapers
cinder blocks or bricks

1. Attitude Check:
TOO MANY ROCKS

Welcome group members and hand out rocks and permanent markers. Ask each member to write on his or her rock one of the things that contributes to divorce.

If necessary, spark members' thinking by offering examples:

- differing religious or political beliefs
- money problems
- boring ruts and routines

When group members have finished writing on their rocks, pile the rocks on the floor in the center of the group circle.

Recruit one male and one female volunteer. Ask these volunteers to play *husband* and *wife*. Offer these directions to this *couple:*

- Together choose one rock from the pile.
- Read aloud what is written on the rock.
- Immediately start discussing the problem on the rock; it's *your* problem, a source of conflict in your marriage. Take different points of view and start disagreeing.

After about 30 seconds, stop the *couple* and ask them to select another rock, adding to their discussion...and their burden. After another 30 seconds, stop the *couple* and ask them to select and add a third rock to the discussion.

Continue in this way for several more minutes, adding additional rocks/topics (burdens) to the *couple* as they continue discussing. Shorten the time between the addition of rocks...20 seconds, 15 second, then 10 seconds. When you sense that the volunteers are feeling overwhelmed, both physically (holding the rocks) and emotionally (dealing with the topics), stop and ask the couple:

- How are you feeling?
- Do you think your marriage can be saved?

Ask the group:

- Do you think this marriage can be saved?
- What has to happen if our *couple* is going to make this marriage work?

2. Attitude Question: DIVORCE

Note: Today's topic may be painfully immediate for one or more group members. Respect members' pain and anger. Don't force members to share if they feel uncomfortable doing so. Be ready to offer extra support one-on-one following the meeting.

Invite group members to share their observations about divorce:
- How many of our parents are divorced? How many of us have friends whose parents are divorced? Is there anyone here whose parents are divorcing *right now?*
- Who would be willing to share their stories about divorce? What happened? Who was involved? How did you feel?
- How do you think God feels about divorce? What does the church say about divorce?
- Are there cases where the home situation is so painful that divorce would be better than staying married? In other words, in your opinion, is divorce ever justified?
- At some level children almost always feel guilty for their parents' divorce; it's important to help children realize that they were *not* the cause.
- What are the results of divorce for those who were married? for their children? for their friends?
- What are the toughest things to deal with if your parents are getting divorced?
- What can married people do to help prevent divorce?
- What can you do *before you get married* to avoid divorce later?

3. Attitude Search: PSALM 27

Distribute Bibles and copies of today's ATTITUDE paper. Divide participants into smaller groups of 3-4 members each. Invite groups to complete the activity God Will Take Care of Me, printed in the papers.

When groups have finished, regather and invite volunteers from each group to share their answers to the final question.

4. Attitude Adjustment: FLIMSY FOUNDATIONS

Make available the old newspapers. Recruit volunteers and invite them to create a "house" of newspapers. As they work, discuss with all group members:
- On what "flimsy foundations" do people sometimes try to build marriages?
- How is this house of newspaper like such a marriage?

When the house is completed, ask group members to place the rocks created in today's Attitude Check on the house, reading each rock aloud as it is placed. The house will probably collapse after the placement of only a few rocks. Discuss:
- What happened to this house—this *marriage*—under the weight of these problems and disagreements?
- Why couldn't this marriage hold up under these problems?

5. Attitude Exit: STRONG FOUNDATIONS

Recruit several new volunteers to construct a second house using bricks or cinder blocks. As they work, ask:
- How is this house of bricks (or blocks) like a solid, lasting marriage?
- What are the building blocks of a strong marriage? *(Ask group members to write their ideas on the bricks or blocks.)*
- How can we include God in the building of a solid marriage?

Again invite group members to place the rocks on the "house," reading each rock as it is placed. This time the house will hold the weight of the rocks. Ask:
- Why does this house—this *marriage*—stand up under problems and disagreements?

Gather for prayer. Invite prayer requests, especially for those experiencing the pain of divorce. Pray:
- Loving God, thanks for loving us... *always.* Divorce hurts. Help us to move through the pain to the promise of your presence with us forever. *Amen.*

a division of Church Publishing Incorporated

600 GRANT ST., #400
DENVER, CO 80203
1.800.824.1813

ATTITUDE

FOR TEENS BY TEENS

DAN'S STORY by Rachel Gluckstern

Dan:

Today as I walked home, I realized that this would be my last night at 1208 Leaf Street. Tomorrow, mom and I will move into an apartment across town, and my dad leaves for Montana. I'm transferring to a new school—never mind the fact it was the middle of the school year and it would be easier to finish at Nelson High than to get new classes—and I'm going to leave the neighborhood that I've lived in almost all of my life.

and turns it upside-down and inside-out. Suddenly, you don't know what to expect or believe.

What do I do now? Wait and pray that things will get better...somehow...sometime.

Leslie:

I watched Dan walk slowly to his house. I know he's moving out tomorrow. I'm going to miss him. It's not fair that Dan has to leave the neighborhood. Why couldn't his parents just get along? I had told him that I would come to visit him and suggested he do the same, but he just sort of shrugged.

My life is totally different now. I guess divorce does that to you. It takes your life that's going fine

(continued on page 2)

1

TRAPPED IN THIS WORLD by Jessica Kirk

My mother thinks she's not beautiful
enough to grace my dad's eyes.
I asked what she meant; I said, "You're beautiful."
"Not to him," she sadly replies.

My dad, you see...he still loves her,
he just doesn't know what he wants out of life.
You can see in his eyes that he loves her;
why can't he stay home and be with his wife?

My mom—she believes in forgiveness
when he asks to forgive him she does.
So why is there always forgiveness?
Ask her this question...she says, "Just because."

My dad can be selfish and hurtful,
but my love has always remained.
Sometimes when he's selfish and hurtful
my mind curses his name.

My mom has a problem with drinking;
she drinks her way out of hard times.
And this problem with drinking
is out of control at times.

And I...I am trapped in this world
my parents have accidentally made.
I am trapped in this world—
it isn't my fault that they're acting this way.

© Copyright 2000
Living the Good News
a division of Church Publishing Incorporated
600 Grant Street
Suite 400
Denver, CO 80203
1 (800) 824-1813

Graphic Design & Illustration:
Carolyn Klass

4

ATTITUDE

GOD WILL TAKE CARE OF ME

THE INSIDE STORY

PSALM 27

A mother calmly explained the word divorce to her five-year-old daughter. "It means that Uncle Jack and Aunt Linda are getting unmarried." The little girl thought about it for a minute, and then blurted out, "But what about Debbie and Ryan? Don't Uncle Jack and Aunt Linda love their children any more?"

Though only five years old, the little girl had a keen understanding of what marriage is all about: a circle of love and commitment that can't be broken without hurting everyone.

Chances are you've been hurt by divorce in someway. Maybe. Maybe it's a part of your own family's experience; maybe it has invaded the lives of other family members or of your friends; maybe it has ravaged your admiration of a mentor or teacher or leader who had an excellent marriage...or so you thought.

It's not the way it was meant to be. A circle, like the wedding ring, has no beginning and no end. So, once marriage becomes divorce, once the circle is snapped, once the sanctuary is ravaged, what happens to the broken pieces?

The psalmist believes that all our feelings of abandonment, of loneliness, of need or of fear are like empty jars that God is longing to fill. The emptier we become, the greater the opportunity.

Listen: "The Lord protects me from all danger; I will never be afraid."

"In times of trouble [God] will shelter me."

"My father and mother may abandon me, but the Lord will take care of me."

"Trust in the Lord. Have faith, do not despair."

A lot of things happen in this life that do not make God happy. Divorce is one of them. But nothing, absolutely nothing, changes God's powerful love, which is always present in our lives and in our parents' lives. That love will triumph.

Your mom comes into your room. From the look on her face, you know something's wrong. "What's up?" you ask, afraid of the answer.

"Your father and I have decided to call it quits. He's moving out tomorrow morning. I think we'll probably get divorced."

You feel like you've been slugged in the gut. You sit on the edge of your bed, stunned. Your emotions whirl around you: hurt, anger, confusion, guilt and a sudden sense of loneliness.

Where do you turn for help? The writer of Psalm 27 faced similar pain. With the members of your small group, read Psalm 27:1-6, then discuss:

• What pain does the writer of Psalm 27 face?

• Where does the writer turn for help to endure that pain?

Read Psalm 27:7-10:

• The writer of Psalm 27 asks God for a bunch of things. Which fit for someone whose parents are divorcing?

• Verse 10 reflects a feeling often felt by teens whose parents divorce. What is that feeling? What is the writer's answer to that feeling?

Read Psalm 27:11-14:

• What final confidence does the writer of Psalm 27 express?

• In general, what comfort and advice does Psalm 27 offer to someone whose parents are divorcing or divorced? (Be ready to share your answers to this question when the larger group regathers.)

DAN'S STORY (continued from page 1)

It's Dan's struggle, not mine. All I can do now is listen and care for him and hope he snaps out of it soon.

Dan:
I saw Leslie right before I left last week. We hugged each other goodbye, both promising to call and visit. Leslie looked so concerned for me. I'm glad that I have a friend who cares. But things are getting better. I thought I'd be lost being in a new school and home without Leslie, but I've found some new friends, and I still can see Leslie when I feel like it. My life has changed forever, but I still have some of my past to depend on, and that's all I need for now.

LEADER'S GUIDE

FOCUS

Transitions: Changes in Relationships

SCRIPTURE

Ecclesiastes 3:1-14

SCAN

Today's meeting explores changing relationships, another area of a teenager's life that often brings painful transitions:
- Attitude Check demonstrates the impact of relationships through a roleplay.
- In Attitude Question, group members discuss their hopes and fears for relationships.
- Attitude Search looks to scripture for encouragement in relationships.
- In Attitude Adjustment, small groups present skits showing how changing relationships affect our lives.
- Attitude Exit invites members to complete summary statements about relationships.

STUFF

Bibles
photocopies of today's paper (pp. 61-62), 1 per participant
role slips (see **before the meeting** note)

Before the meeting prepare role slips for Attitude Check. On separate slips of paper, copy each of these roles:
- whiny friend at school
- coach upset because student isn't committed enough
- strict mother or father
- supportive best friend
- younger sister or brother who looks up to student
- bullying older sister or brother
- favorite teacher who likes this student a lot
- teacher who doesn't respect this student much

- ex-girlfriend or ex-boyfriend carrying a grudge
- demanding current girlfriend or current boyfriend
- loving grandparent
- worried pastor

Prepare one slip for each participant, *minus one*. If you have a large group, add other roles or conduct the activity with smaller groups.

1. Attitude Check: TONS 'O RELATIONSHIPS

Welcome group members and recruit one volunteer to play the part of the *student* in a roleplay. Ask all other group members to select a role slip prepared **before the meeting**. Explain:
- The volunteer is a *student*, struggling—like all of us—to handle all the different relationships in life—at school, home, church and with friends.
- The rest of us are the different people in the *student's* life. We each have our own special relationship to the *student*, indicated on our slips. And, as we can also see on our slips, we all have different *attitudes* toward the *student*.
- In a moment, we will interact with the *student*, sharing what we're thinking and feeling, and above all, responding to what we've heard the *student* saying to the others of us who share a relationship with the *student*.
- Be as outspoken and creative as you wish.

Invite group members to stand together in a circle. Ask the *student* to move, person by person, around the circle, interacting with each person for 20-30 seconds. As necessary, remind members to stay in their roles. You might also encourage members to address the ways previously enacted roles affect their roles; for example:

ATTITUDE FOR TEENS BY TEENS

- An ex-boyfriend might say, "We break up for one week and already you're seeing someone new! How do you think that makes *me* feel?"
- An unfriendly teacher might say, "You're not here in school for sports or friends; you're here to get an education!"

When the *student* has interacted with every member, continue with Attitude Question.

2. Attitude Question: SORTING OUT

Invite the *student* in today's opening activity to discuss his or her role:
- To what extent did this feel like real life?
- Describe your feelings as you went around the circle. Did you feel pressured? annoyed? frustrated?
- To what extent did your role as the *student* become increasingly complicated?

Ask the other members to discuss:
- To what extent did this mirror what happens in all our lives? How often do we feel the pressure of competing relationships? of changing relationships?
- How did the *student* change as he (or she) proceeded around the circle? How did his (or her) responses change? his (or her) attitude?
- In what ways do changing relationships bring change to our lives?
- What changes have relationships brought to your family? to your life at school? to other friendships?
- How have your relationships changed how you feel about yourself? about God?

3. Attitude Search: ECCLESIASTES 3:1-14

Distribute Bibles and turn together to Ecclesiastes 3:1-14. Divide participants into two groups; read verse 1 in unison, then read verses 2-8 responsively by dividing each line into two parts, one group reading the first part of each line, the other group the second, like this:
- *first group:* He sets the time for birth...

- *second group:* ...and the time for death,
- *first group:* the time for planting...
- *second group:* ...and the time for pulling up.

After finishing verse 8, discuss:
- What is the point of these verses?
- Which verses relate to relationships?

While some of the verse have obvious meaning for relationships, challenge group members to go further; for example:
- In friendship, when is there a time to "find"? a time to "lose" or let go?
- In families, when is the time for "tearing"? when for "mending"?

Ask group members to read silently the remaining portion of today's reading, verses 9-14. Discuss:
- When facing ever-changing relationships, what advice can we find in these verses? what comfort?

4. Attitude Adjustment: CHANGE SKITS

Divide participants into smaller groups of 5-8 members each. Distribute copies of today's ATTITUDE paper. Ask each group to complete the activity Always Changing, printed in the papers.

When groups are ready, ask them to present their skits to the other groups.

5. Attitude Exit: COPING

Gather group members in a circle. Invite volunteers to complete this statement:
- A very valuable relationship in my life is...because...

When all who wish to complete the statement have done so, invite volunteers to complete this statement:
- One way I can cope with changing relationships is...

Close by praying:
- Loving God, thanks for all the people you've given us to love and relate to. Help us to do that well. *Amen.*

a division of
Church Publishing
Incorporated

600 Grant St., #400
Denver, CO 80203
1.800.824.1813

CHANGES IN RELATIONSHIPS

ATTITUDE
FOR TEENS BY TEENS

A TALE   by Jared Crain

Ahh. How refreshing. The first day of school on a warm, late August morning. Our friend, Joe, awoke to the sound of his alarm radio. Today is young Joseph's first day of high school.

Today could have been a nice day, an exciting day for the boy; but Joe had just moved from one school district to another just two weeks earlier.

Moving away from a familiar neighborhood filled with the familiar faces of good friends, Joe moved to a new neighborhood where the only faces he knew were those of his parents.

At school, Joe missed the company of his friends and that of those

cute girls last year in eighth grade. In short, Joe's exciting day at a new school quickly turned into a frightening experience, an experience of loneliness and despair. He'd been stripped of his old, comfortable relationships; he'd been dumped into a new world of relationships.

Without the company of those he knew and could relate to, the familiar world of classes and lunch and studying and meeting in the hallway had twisted into a nightmare. He wanted to quit. None of the other students looked cool...just scary. Everyone he saw was not a person. They were just there. They were *them*.

Change. Transition. Confusion. Pain.

THEY CHANGE OUR HEARTS
by Lori VanDeman

If you listen to the radio, you've heard love songs and broken-heart songs. You've heard about loving and losing, gaining and growing, great love, missed love and unfulfilled love.

At one time or another you might have felt like they've been written just for you. At other times you've regarded them as silly or shallow.

There may be more to these songs than meets the ear.

Love songs are about *relationships*, expressing the feelings and thoughts and fears and

joys of people in or out of relationships. Their relationships made enough of a difference in their lives for them to write songs about them.

Think about a relationship of yours...parent, friend, relative, whatever. How has this relationship influenced you? New emotions, fresh discoveries about yourself, even those catchy little phrases that you can't get out of your head—they all count. For instance, I still remember my uncle teaching me how to "magically" pull off my finger, and even now I still find occasion to use that particular "skill."

Nearly every encounter we have with other people makes a change in us. The people we know may teach us something new or perhaps lend a few encouraging words. They teach us how to tie our shoes, tell a joke or see something deeper in ourselves. God puts people in our lives—gives us *relationships*—for a reason. Our relationships accomplish God's purpose. They change our hearts.

© Copyright 2000
Living the Good News
a division of Church Publishing Incorporated
600 Grant Street
Suite 400
Denver, CO 80203
1 (800) 824-1813

Graphic Design & Illustration:
Carolyn Klass

ATTITUDE

Living the Good News

ALWAYS CHANGING

Our relationships are always changing...and always bringing change.

Sometimes those changes are tough to handle.

With the members of your group, choose one of the following situations to present as a skit for the other groups.

1 A new romance: This is it! The person you've been waiting for. You can't spend enough time together. But what happens at home? with other friends? at school?

2 A new baby: Today the adoption agency brings over your new baby sister. You're glad she'll be a part of your family, but what changes will this bring for you and your brother? How will it change your relationship to your parents?

3 A new best friend: Your previous best friend betrayed your trust. Now you've found someone new. Lots to talk about. Lots to discover about each other. What happens to your other friendships?

4 A new attitude: You've been a loner most of your life, but recently you've started coming out of your shell. You're making friends at school...even dating. But the changed you is hard for your family to deal with. How do they cope with your new interests outside of home?

In your skit, show how a shift in one relationship demands adjustments (not always easy ones) in other relationships.

Use all the members of your group in your skit.

ECCLESIASTES 3:1-14

THE

INSIDE STORY

How odd it is the way we drift in and out of each others' lives, clinging and loving and needing and then letting go, out of sight and out of mind. How does that happen?

We humans are curious about this fluidity, this movement of time on our deepest feelings. We laugh about it when we watch sitcoms that poke fun at the on-again-off-again nature of our friendships; we cry about it when they are dramatized for us as mini-series; we are enthralled by it when they are exaggerated on soap operas.

Still, it's odd. Your best friend in elementary school no longer acknowledges you in the hall. You and your junior high buddy don't have anything in common any more. When you graduate from high school, the ones you miss the most will surely fade from your affections, if not your memory. Then, someday, you won't recognize your dearest college friends at a reunion. We're blessed if we keep even one friend for a lifetime.

The reading from Ecclesiastes consoles us in our losses. The author explains to us that as humans we must accept the changes that space and time bring us. But it feels uncomfortable because God has set eternity in our hearts. We see it; we reach for it; but it is not ours, at least for now. Only God is eternal, constant, unchanging.

Ecclesiastes' advice is good: Enjoy the friends you have. They may not remain forever. Do not think of it as losing love, but as gathering and storing love. For "everything God does will last forever." When your friendships change and seem to pass away, know that what was good and right and perfect in them, what was created by God, will remain. A time will come...

Enjoy the friends you have. They may not remain forever.

LEADER'S GUIDE

FOCUS

Transitions: Dedicating Yourself to God

SCRIPTURE

Genesis 22:1-19

SCAN

Today's meeting explores the changes we experience when we commit ourselves to God:
- In Attitude Check, group members create a commitment collage.
- Attitude Question examines what it means to dedicate oneself to God.
- In Attitude Search, members take a look at Abraham's remarkable commitment to God.
- Attitude Adjustment guides members through a meditation on Christian commitment.
- In Attitude Exit, members draw their commitments to God.

STUFF

Bibles
photocopies of today's paper (pp. 65-66), 1 per participant
magazines with pictures and advertising
large sheet of poster board
glue
drawing paper
colored pencils or crayons

1. Attitude Check:
COMMITMENT COLLAGE

Welcome group members. Make available the old magazines, the poster board and glue. Offer members these instructions:
- Look through the magazines for pictures that you think are examples of dedication or commitment.

- If you can, select pictures that reflect dedication or commitment in your own life.
- Tear out these pictures and be ready to explain why you chose them.

When each group member has found two or three pictures, invite volunteers to show their pictures to the group and tell why they chose them. Ask members to assemble the pictures into a collage, gluing the pictures onto the poster board. Title the collage appropriately.

2. Attitude Question:
TALKING COMMITMENT

Invite group members to discuss:
- What is *dedication? commitment?*
- To what things are we dedicated? To what people are we committed? what objects? what ideas? what pastimes? what goals?
- Why are we committed to these things? What makes them worthy of our dedication?
- What does it mean to be dedicated to God?
    — How is dedication to God shown?
    — What's involved in dedicating your life to God? What new things might you take on? What might you give up? What things might change?
    — What are the benefits that come from a life lived for God?
    — How does your dedication to God affect those around you?
- Think of your own level of commitment to God:
    — What changes have come about in your life due to your dedication to God? When have these changes been easy? difficult?
    — Who has helped you deal with and accept the changes that following God has brought to your life?
- Let's look in scripture at an amazing example of commitment to God.

3. Attitude Search: GENESIS 22:1-19

Distribute Bibles and copies of today's ATTITUDE paper. Invite group members individually to complete the activity Now *That's* Commitment!, printed in the papers. (For members unfamiliar with scripture, explain that they will find Genesis at the very beginning of the Bible.)

When group members have completed the activity, regather and discuss:

● In the story of Abraham and Isaac, it's clear that Abraham loved Isaac a lot, but that Abraham loved God more.
● In our lives, do we love God "the most"? Explain.
● How might God know if we loved God more than everything else in our lives?

4. Attitude Adjustment: MEDITATION

Invite group members to close their eyes. Ask them to sit quietly and comfortably as you lead them through this guided meditation. Pause where indicated:

● It's late at night as you sit alone in your bedroom studying. It's raining outside; you hear the rain hit the window, and you smell the damp earth outside. You feel peaceful and a little sleepy. Enjoy the rain and the quiet of your room. *(Pause.)*
● Suddenly you sense you are not alone. You look up, and see a stranger sitting on the edge of your bed. Amazingly, you feel no fear. "Who are you?" you ask. Picture the stranger in your mind's eye. *(Pause.)*
● The stranger smiles and says, "I am Jesus." What are your first feelings? your first thoughts? *(Pause.)*
● "I've come to answer one question for you. What question would you like to ask me?" Jesus asks. You think about all the things you've wanted to ask God...about life, about death, about sadness, about the future...it's hard to pick one question. *(Pause.)*

● Finally, you've chosen your question. Go ahead and ask it. *(Pause.)*
● Jesus answers. Listen to his answer. *(Pause.)*
● You thank Jesus for the answer to your question, and then he says, "I love you and I want you to follow me. I want you to be with me, know me, love me. Will you follow me?" You hear his question. Observe how you feel. Listen to your thoughts. *(Pause.)*
● Finally, hesitantly, you answer. In the quietness of your own heart, what do you say to Jesus? *(Pause.)*
● After you answer, Jesus gives you a hug. "Thanks," you hear him whisper. You are alone again. *(Pause.)*

Allow a minute of silence before asking group members to open their eyes. Invite volunteers to share their meditation experience, though expect that most members may be too quieted to say much.

Continue with Attitude Exit.

5. Attitude Exit: COMMITMENT

Distribute a sheet of drawing paper to each group member. Make available the colored pencils or crayons. Explain:

● Draw the response you gave to Christ in the meditation we just completed.
● Your drawing can be symbolic or literal ...whatever makes sense to *you*.
● Only volunteers will be asked to share their drawings.

Give group members several minutes to complete their drawings, then invite volunteers *only* to show and explain their finished artwork.

Close by praying:

● God, thank you for being totally dedicated to us, no matter how dedicated we might be to you. Draw us to you, God. *Amen.*

a division of
Church Publishing
Incorporated

600 GRANT ST., #400
DENVER, CO 80203
1.800.824.1813

DEDICATING YOURSELF TO GOD

ATTITUDE
FOR TEENS BY TEENS

EMPTY YOUR WORRIED THOUGHTS
by Jessica Kirk

Empty your worried thoughts
and be filled with life;
nail your sins to the cross
and be lifted up to Christ.

Close your eyes and take a step;
you'll land on solid ground,
for the light you find in him,
will lead you, heaven-bound.

The journey you embark upon
will be hard and satisfying.
Dedication to the Christ will save you
in the moment you are dying.

For he will gently hold you in his arms
and carry you up Jacob's ladder,
into his kingdom he will take you
and give you to his Father.

MORE THAN THAT   *by Lori VanDeman*

I've been a Christian my whole life. Going to church was part of the routine. When I wanted something, I'd say a quick prayer. I was a Christian, but now I think it was little more than in name. Christianity seemed to have little real bearing on my life. I got through the days just for the day's sake. I was a friend to my friends and nameless face to everyone else. No bond was too strong to be broken, but it didn't really matter.

Now I think being a Christian is much more than that.

I was invited by a girl in one of my classes to attend her youth group. I accepted, not sure what to expect. What I found there opened my eyes. These people were unlike anyone else I'd ever met. They were genuine people. I had never met any of them before, yet with them I felt loved. They openly rejoiced in their relationship to God. They spoke avidly of all God had done in their lives. I felt inspired.

And not only that, they *wanted* me to join them. So I did, and it was the greatest thing I've ever done for myself. I now feel the burning love that God feels for me. I see how God

(continued on page 2)

© Copyright 2000
Living the Good News
a division of Church Publishing Incorporated
600 Grant Street
Suite 400
Denver, CO 80203
1 (800) 824-1813

Graphic Design & Illustration:
Carolyn Klass

ATTITUDE

Living the Good News

NOW *THAT'S* COMMITMENT!

Boy, talk about your commitment! Abraham wins, no contest. Few people have demonstrated the depth of commitment to God that we see in this simple story from Genesis.

Start by reading just Genesis 22:1-2. Stop and ask yourself:

- What incredible thing is God asking of Abraham?
- Why does God ask this of Abraham?

Now read the next portion of the story in Genesis 22:3-10. Ask yourself:

- How is Abraham demonstrating his commitment to God?
- When in our lives might God ask for this kind of commitment?

Now finish the story in Genesis 22:11-19. Ask yourself:

- How does the story of Abraham and Isaac end?
- How does God reward Abraham for his commitment?

MORE THAN THAT *(continued from page 1)*

you to answer the call to dedicate yourself to Christ. If you haven't already, open your eyes, open your heart, open your life. God is there, waiting for *you*.

God loves *everyone* with a burning love—including *you*. God longs for

works in my everyday life. Being a Christian is far more than what I used to know or imagine.

THE

INSIDE STORY

Humans have an incredible capacity for intensity in every aspect of life. We rarely use it.

A lot of people exercise. Some are into sports. A few could be considered athletes. And then there are the Olympians, men and women who have dedicated themselves to the perfect discipline of their bodies.

A lot of people study. Some are really into learning. A few could be considered intellectuals. And then there are the scholars, men and women who have dedicated themselves to the perfect discipline of their minds.

Most of us are not very intense about anything much.

A lot of people believe in God. Some are pretty religious. A few could be considered active and sincere Christians. And then there are the saints, living men and women who have dedicated all of themselves to the perfect love of God.

People admire athletes and Olympians; people esteem intellectuals and scholars; people sneer at saints. They use words like *fanatics, loonies, extremists*. If they're conservative, they're called fundamentalists. If they're liberal, they're called radicals. Either way, we reduce them to a label.

Abraham is a saint. He begins by listening to God's voice. He then takes a step into the unknown by leaving his home for a place God would show him. He then pushes his faith further, trusting God for a son even though he and Sarah were way past childbearing age.

In today's reading we see how far Abraham's dedication to God will go. It pushes all the limits. He gives up the son he loves; he lets go of God's promises about an heir; he puts his relationship with Sarah on the line; he risks it all; he withholds nothing. Why? Because Abraham is dedicated completely to God.

You're past the place of mere believing. You're past the point of getting serious about your faith. God invites you to be a saint.

LEADER'S GUIDE

FOCUS

Transitions: Death

SCRIPTURE

Revelation 21:1-7

SCAN

Today's meeting explores the changes brought to our lives by death:
- Attitude Check invites group members to write their own obituaries.
- In Attitude Question, members discuss their experiences with and ideas about death.
- In Attitude Search, members respond with artwork to a scriptural vision of life after death.
- Attitude Adjustment asks small groups to compose acrostic poems about death and the afterlife.
- Attitude Exit urges group members to let today's discussion of death move them to take care of "unfinished business" in their lives.

STUFF

Bibles
photocopies of today's paper (pp. 69-70), 1 per participant
pens or pencils
paper
chalkboard and chalk or newsprint and marker
drawing paper
colored pencils or pastel crayons
modeling clay
watercolor paper, paints and brushes
jars of water
paper towels

1. Attitude Check: OBITUARIES

Welcome group members and distribute paper and pens or pencils. Make this announcement:
- We've just learned that every one of us in this room has a fatal disease. We only have two weeks to live.
- Knowing that we will die in two weeks gives us a unique opportunity: we can write our own obituaries!
- An obituary is a tribute to yourself telling everyone what you'd like to be remembered for.
- Your obituary need not be long, just a few sentences.

Give group members time to complete their obituaries, then invite volunteers to read their obituaries aloud. When all who wish to read their obituaries aloud have done so, discuss:
- How could living daily with the awareness of what we've written in our obituaries help us to live more fully?
- How could living daily with what's in our obituaries better prepare us for our own deaths?

2. Attitude Question: ON DEATH

Invite group members to share further thoughts and feelings about death:
- Define *death*. What is it?
- What have we experienced with death?
  — What feelings has our experience with death brought out? What hopes? questions? fears?
  — How have we handled these feelings and questions?
  — What changes has death brought to our lives?
- Why is death feared? What about death frightens us? fascinates us?
- What things can ease the pain of death?

ATTITUDE FOR TEENS BY TEENS

- To what extent do we think about our own deaths? How often? What worries us most about our own deaths?
- Where do you think death comes in God's plans for us?
- What do you believe about life after death?
- Let's look at something the Bible says about life after death.

3. Attitude Search: REVELATION 21:1-7

Distribute Bibles and invite group members to turn together to Revelation 21:1-7. (If necessary, point out that Revelation is the last book in the Bible.) Explain to members that the book of Revelation is a highly symbolic description of heaven and the life to come.

Invite volunteers to read Revelation 21:1-7 aloud, each volunteer reading several verses. After the reading, ask group members to offer single word descriptions of what heaven will be like, according to Revelation 21. Challenge members to come up with at least 20 single words, for example:
- joyful
- healing
- satisfying

Ask a volunteer to write group members' words on chalkboard or newsprint. When finished with the list, ask a volunteer to reread aloud Revelation 21:14. Make available the drawing paper, colored pencils or pastel crayons, modeling clay, watercolor paper, paints and brushes, jars of water and paper towels. Explain:
- Create a piece of artwork that reflects your personal vision of heaven. Choose from drawing, sculpting or painting.
- You can use the images of Revelation 21, but you can also create your own.
- Let your artwork be symbolic or literal, whichever you like.

Give plenty of time for group members to complete their artwork, then invite volunteers to show and explain their finished pieces to the group.

4. Attitude Adjustment: ACROSTIC POEMS

Divide participants into small groups of 3-4 members each. Distribute copies of today's ATTITUDE paper and ask groups to complete the activity Death and the Afterlife, printed in the papers.

When groups have finished their poems, regather and ask volunteers from each group to read their poems aloud to the other groups. Discuss:
- How does death change us? How does death change the way we feel? think? view our lives?
- What resources do we have to help us cope with the changes brought by death? to help *others* cope with these changes?
- In what ways can our understanding of heaven and life after death help us to cope with death?

5. Attitude Exit: UNFINISHED BUSINESS

Distribute additional paper and explain:
- Let's go back to the fact that we're all going to die in two weeks.
- One advantage of this was being able to write our own obituaries. Another advantage is this: We can take care of unfinished business, thanking people we've forgotten to thank, apologizing where we need to apologize, asking last questions we've avoided asking, saying "I love you," etc.
- Write down three or four items of business you'd like to take care of before you die.

When group members have finished their lists, challenge them to consider actually taking care of these items this week. Close by praying:
- God, thanks for the assurance of eternal life. Help us deal with the changes brought by death and dying. And help us be ready, now, to finish business with those we love. What good will waiting do? *Amen.*

a division of Church Publishing Incorporated

600 GRANT ST., #400 DENVER, CO 80203 1.800.824.1813

DEATH

ATTITUDE

FOR TEENS BY TEENS

THE DEATH OF BECKY
by Jessica Kirk

The last day I saw Becky I had my hair cut short. I would run my hands through it to realize just how very short it was. On that day, I would realize that life could be cut short too.

Becky lived in a house over on Zinnia Street with her husband, my great-uncle Paul. In that house Becky had kept a home and a family. She was a beautiful artist. She could paint country landscapes and it would look like God was in her paintbrush. She kept her paintings in her house, and in her house she held me as she died.

With my head resting comfortably in her lap, I listened as she consoled

me. She told me that I was beautiful, and that she loved me. Her frail hands, her alive fingers lovingly stroked my hair, gently sweeping it from my face. She looked ghostly white and fragile as china. Her face was solemn, but her eyes were not sad. I had never seen her this weak, nor this beautiful.

She asked, "Has your headache passed? Is there anything else I can do to help?" This woman, who was dying from a brain tumor, was worried about my little headache. I marveled at her selflessness. She struggled just to sit up, yet with ease

(continued on page 4)

RELEASE
by Lorie VanDeman

From spirit
to body
   to soul
we change, we undergo
   a metamorphosis.
Like a cocoon our bodies encase us,
   not sure of the beauty inside.
When our moment of death
   comes upon us,
   we release a butterfly.

Death is not the end of the road;
instead it becomes a toll
   paid for you in full
     by the cross.
The cross is the key
   to the springtime
where the butterfly
   floats on the breeze.

Embrace the change
   that you come to,
for out of your body
   you're free.

THE DEATH OF BECKY
(continued from page 1)

could make me feel comfortable. Even with death at hand, Becky gave of herself and of her life. I left that day at peace, one in mind, body and spirit.

At Becky's funeral I didn't cry. I knew that I would miss her, and I knew that I would always remember her; but I was not sad about her death. She had said goodbye to me in her own way. She had given me some wonderful, gracious part of herself—and I would carry that with me always.

ATTITUDE

Living the Good News

DEATH AND THE AFTERLIFE

Death. We read about it in the newspapers. We see it depicted on TV and in movies. Many of us have had friends, relatives or pets die. Some of us may have seen someone die in a car accident or by a gunshot.

The reality of death is frightening, final, painful, lonely, mysterious.

With the members of your small group, compose a five-line acrostic poem about death that reflects your real feelings and thoughts. If possible, include God somewhere in your poem.

Let each line of the poem start with a different letter of the word *death:*

D

E

A

T

H

Heaven. What is it *really*? So many people have described it in so many different ways—peace, laughter, reunion, light, companionship, celebration. What's *your* view of heaven?

With the members of your small group, compose a six-line poem about heaven and the afterlife. Again, include God somewhere in your poem. Let each line being with a different letter of the word *heaven.*

H

E

A

V

E

N

THE [ ] INSIDE STORY

REVELATION 21:1-7

Space is not the final frontier; death is. Someday we will all become explorers.

We can guess about death; we can entertain rumors of those who have glimpsed it and returned; we can talk about stages of grief and about time healing all wounds. But when you bury someone you love, you need more than that.

God does not give us details about death and resurrection and what happens to the spirit in between. God does give us certain promises: that in Christ all will be made alive (1 Corinthians 15:22); that the dead in Christ will rise and that we will be reunited with them (1 Thessalonians 4:16-17).

Today's reading from Revelation reminds us that death is not permanent. God has a goal: to live among us; to rid creation of all the old things, like death and crying and pain; to "wipe away all tears from our eyes."

What does this image do to your soul when it weeps uncontrollably: God stoops down, takes a handkerchief from a pocket, gently lifts your chin and wipes your tears? What does this say about God? about what God wants for you? about what God wants for those whom you love?

When you face death, when its cold fingers pry open your pleasant life and squeeze out all the joy and love and hope so that everything is broken and empty and over, then rest in God, who not only holds those we have loved and lost, but keeps them for a future day. To that brightest of all meetings, bring us!

God has a goal: to live among us; to rid creation of all the old things, like death and crying and pain; to "wipe away all tears from our eyes."

LEADERS' GUIDE

FOCUS

Ethics: Gossip

SCRIPTURE

James 3:1-12

SCAN

Today's meeting explores gossip:
- In Attitude Check, group members illustrate gossip with the classic game of Gossip.
- In Attitude Question, members define gossip and discuss the harm it does.
- Attitude Search uncovers some pointed advice about gossip in the epistle of James.
- In Attitude Adjustment, members practice confronting and stopping gossip.
- Group members pledge to do less gossiping in today's Attitude Exit.

STUFF

Bibles
photocopies of today's paper (pp. 73-74), 1 per participant
pens or pencils
pad of paper
chalkboard and chalk or newsprint and marker

1. Attitude Check: GOSSIP

Welcome group members and invite them to arrange their chairs in a large circle. Lead members in a game of Gossip:
- The leader begins by whispering a message into the ear of the player seated to the left. That player repeats the message, whispering it to the next player. Play continues in this manner around the circle.
- Each player may say the message *only once* to the next player; no repeating or clarification is allowed. The player repeats exactly what he or she thinks was heard.

- Play continues until the message has been passed around the circle to the player seated to the right of the leader. This final player says the message aloud. The leader then says the original message aloud.

Here are possible messages:
- Shabana slipped on Shep the chef's shiny new soup server.
- Tiny Tim took Tina's tutu and tossed it in a tree.
- Nate knocked his knuckles on Neil's nubby noggin.
- Pip poked his protruding proboscis painfully into Pam's plate of purple pickles.

Invite volunteers to invent and start additional messages. Continue playing as long as group members enjoy themselves, then move on to Attitude Question.

2. Attitude Question: UNDERSTANDING GOSSIP

Invite group members to discuss their game of Gossip:
- What happened to most (or all) of our messages?
- What does the game of Gossip illustrate about how a story about someone changes as it's passed from person to person?
- Relate a time when something that was true about you became twisted as people passed it along.
- What is *gossip*?
  — How do we recognize gossip?
  — What different forms does gossip take?
- Why do people gossip?
  — What does gossip do for those who gossip?
  — What do we have to lose if we stop gossiping?
- What's the result of gossip? What can result for the one who gossips? for the one who is gossiped about?

● At what point does sharing information become gossip?

3. Attitude Search: JAMES 3:1-12

Divide participants into smaller groups of 3-4 members each. Distribute pens or pencils and copies of today's ATTITUDE paper. Invite groups to complete the activity The Tongue, printed in the papers.

When groups have finished their discussions, regather and discuss:
● What new images did your group invent to show the power of the tongue?
● What examples of the power of the tongue did your group think of?

4. Attitude Adjustment: CONFRONTING GOSSIP

Recruit eight volunteers and ask them to stand in a line in the center of the group. Hand the first person in line a pen or pencil and a pad of paper. Offer these instructions to the volunteers:
● As we did in the opening game, we're going to illustrate the workings of gossip.
● The first person in the line writes on the pad a simple sentence describing something *positive* and *true* about the eighth and final person in the line. The sentence should be no more than 10 words long, for example: *Kai works out three days a week at home.*
● The first person then passes the pad to the second person in the line, who changes *just one word* in the sentence on the pad.
● Play continues down the line, with volunteers three through seven each changing *just one word* in the sentence.
● When the pad gets to the final person in line, he or she reads it aloud, but here is where this activity differs from the first. At this point, volunteer eight steps to the

front of the line and confronts the first volunteer on the final form of what is written on the pad, saying, for example, "I heard you said this: What's going on?"
● The final volunteer moves down the line of volunteers, finding out how, where and why the story changed, setting the record straight and "clearing his or her name."

Repeat the activity with other volunteers. Then discuss:
● In what way does this activity illustrate how and why stories shift as they're told and retold?
● In what way does this activity model for us a way to confront and deal with gossip as it happens to us or others around us?
● In what way does this activity encourage us to question the truth of stories-in-progress and to stop their spread?
● In what way does this activity demonstrate the importance of talking directly with others?

5. Attitude Exit: PLEDGE

Write the title *Stopping Gossip* on chalkboard or newsprint. Beneath the title write *direct communication*. Ask:
● How else can we stop gossiping?
  — How else can we stop *ourselves* from gossiping?
  — How else can we stop gossip from other people?

Ask a volunteer to add suggestions to the list on chalkboard or newsprint.

Close the session by inviting group members to pledge to cut down on gossiping. Offer each group member an opportunity to complete this pledge/prayer:
● Dear God, who only says the truth in love, this week I pledge not to gossip when...

a division of
Church Publishing
Incorporated

600 GRANT ST., #400
DENVER, CO 80203
1.800.824.1813

GOSSIP

RESPECT IS THE KEY
by Jerry Berg

friendship could be threatened or that a reputation could be damaged, stop.

What can you do about gossip? First, think before you speak. Consider your source: How reliable was it? How close to the subject are they? Consider the consequences: Will your telling this story upset anyone if they knew about it? Consider the need: Is there a point to telling the story? Will it help someone? Make people feel better? The first step to stopping gossip is to think first.

(continued on page 2)

Sometimes the topic of your conversations drifts away from the immediate participants. You start talking about friends and acquaintances. Then you may start talking about what someone said about someone else getting in trouble because someone told someone else that...*stop right there!*

You're crossing into gossip territory. If the story you're telling came second- or thirdhand, think twice about telling it. As stories are passed from person to person, facts get distorted. If there's even a slight chance that someone could get hurt, that a

DID YOU HEAR?
by Rachel Gluckstern

"Did you hear? Steve got caught drinking with his sister smashed on vodka by his girlfriend Pam who was all over Josh at the time. They haven't spoken to each other all week. Pam told Katie and Paul overheard and told Mark who told Sandy who slipped accidentally so Darrin found out along with Kendra who went directly to Sam who just told me. But it's a secret, so don't tell, okay?"

Having heard convoluted stories before, I was disinclined to believe this one, except for the fact that Pam told Steve if she ever caught him drinking again they were through. Being Steve's buddy (sort of) I felt obliged to ask Steve what was up.

"Hey Steve, heard what happened—that's rough man."

Steve didn't seem particularly surprised I had heard. "More embarrassing than anything else—especially for my sister."

"How's Pam doing?"

Steve looked thoughtful. "I haven't been able to talk to her all week. As far as I could tell, she was slightly amused. Other then that, she doesn't really care."

That threw me. "But I thought you guys were through if she ever caught you drinking again."

Now Steve was surprised. "Who said anything about *me* drinking?"

I repeated what I had heard.

"Who said *that*? What idiots! What happened was Pam and I caught my sister smashed and all over Josh. How did it turn into what you heard?"

"No clue."

Feeling it was my duty to tell the truth and nothing but the truth, I tried to correct the rumor. Unfortunately the stories got twisted together, which made things worse so I gave up and stepped out of the gossip mill.

"Did you hear...?"

"Not interested."

© copyright 2000
Living the Good News
a division of Church Publishing Incorporated
600 Grant Street
Suite 400
Denver, CO 80203
1 (800) 824-1813

Graphic Design & Illustration:
Carolyn Klass

ATTITUDE

THE TONGUE

(A Guide for Small-Group Exploration)

1. With the members of your small group, read James 3:1-6 aloud. You could take turns reading verses, have one volunteer read the whole thing, or divide into two smaller groups and alternate reading verses.

2. In verses 1-6, James compares the tongue to three different things:
   — a small bit used to guide a large horse
   — a small rudder that steers a huge ship
   — a tiny flame that grows into a forest-destroying fire

   What do all these images have in common?

3. With your group, think up another one or two images that communicate the same idea about the tongue...how something very small can have a huge effect well beyond its size.

4. Now read James 3:7-12. (Choose a method, just like before.)

5. When have you seen "the tongue" used for great good? When have you seen "the tongue" used for great evil?

6. When have you seen "the tongue" used for giving thanks to God? When have you seen "the tongue" used for cursing other people?

RESPECT (continued from page 1)

Second, if someone else is gossiping, change the subject. If the subject can't be changed, ask some pointed questions, like, "Are you sure about that? Is that what was really said? Do you think there's a reason why she feels that way?"

And third, the best way to stop gossip from spreading is not to repeat the story yourself.

Respect for others is the key to stopping gossip. Respect people's privacy, feelings and beliefs. They'll do the same for you.

JAMES 3:1-12

THE _____

INSIDE STORY

A horse's bit. A ship's rudder. A small spark. A poisonous fang. A strange mix of images, seemingly insignificant in the big picture, but their size disguises their immense power.

A bit: a small piece of steel that turns a horse; a rudder: a flat piece of metal attached to the bottom of a boat's stern that forces the entire ship to move in a different direction; a spark: a flicker of fire that can begin a flame which consumes everything; the fang: a grooved tooth in a slithering wild animal that can kill.

James tells us that the tongue is like this: small and enormously useful, but wild and dangerous and powerful. With it we can sing and share ourselves with others and encourage friends and communicate needs. With it we can gossip and spread hate and humiliate and offend others. How can this be? How can one small part of our bodies become an instrument both of worship and of war?

Our tongues bring up what is deep in our hearts. When we gossip, we're telling the truth, not about the other person, but about us. When we gossip, giving our tongues free rein, we only reveal the malice, hardheartedness, resentment, anger and insecurities we have inside. Our tongue both betrays us and hurts others.

And the strange thing is that the less we control our tongue, using it for evil instead of good, the more powerful and unruly and savage it becomes.

Next time your tongue is itching to wag, use the old taming rule: Is it kind? Is it true? Is it necessary? If you can't say yes to all three questions, bite it.

> How can one small part of our bodies become an instrument both of worship and of war?

LEADERS' GUIDE

FOCUS

Ethics: Lying

SCRIPTURE

Genesis 20

SCAN

Today's meeting looks at lying:
- Attitude Check introduces the difficulty of getting truth from a "compulsive liar."
- In Attitude Question, group members complete a lying inventory.
- In Attitude Search, small groups explore an Old Testament story of lying.
- Members weave a "web of deceit" in today's Attitude Adjustment.
- In Attitude Exit, members pledge to tell the truth in the coming week.

STUFF

Bibles
photocopies of today's paper (pp. 77-78), 1 per participant
pens or pencils
ball of string or twine
large scissors

Before the meeting recruit a quick-thinking volunteer to take the role of a *compulsive liar* in today's Attitude Check. Prepare the *liar* by explaining:
- Your job will be to answer all questions with lies.
- The "truth" that you are trying to hide is this: There is a fire starting in the next room of the building.
- It will be the group's job to get this "truth" out of you.

1. Attitude Check: THE LIAR

Welcome group members and introduce your volunteer:

- This is *(name of volunteer)*. She (or he) is a compulsive liar. Nothing she (or he) says is the truth.
- She (or he) knows something extremely important for us to know. We've got to get it out of her (or him).
- I'll begin by asking the first question: "Is there an emergency somewhere?"

When the group has either figured out the emergency or given up in frustration, continue with Attitude Question.

2. Attitude Question: I *NEVER* LIE!

Invite group members to discuss:
- What problems were caused by the volunteer's lies?

Distribute pens or pencils and copies of today's ATTITUDE paper. Ask group members to complete the Truth and Lie Inventory, printed in the papers. Ask group members to put their names somewhere on the back cover of the papers.

When group members have finished, collect their papers and tally the scores for each item on the inventory. Return members' papers and read the results of the inventory, item by item. As appropriate, allow time for discussion after each item. You could ask, for example:
- Are you surprised by our answers to this item? Explain.
- What do we learn about ourselves from our answers to this question?
- Was it difficult or easy to answer this question? Explain.

After reviewing the inventory, discuss:
- Define *lying*.
- Why do people lie? What does lying accomplish?
- What are the results of lying for the liar? for those lied to?
- How do we know when people are lying to us?

ATTITUDE FOR TEENS BY TEENS

- Is lying ever okay? Explain.
- Share some personal stories about lying and its consequences.
- What's the difference, if any, between lies, fibs and half-truths?
- If you were to make a case for "always telling the truth," what would you say?

3. Attitude Search: GENESIS 20

Distribute Bibles and invite group members to turn to Genesis 20. Recruit volunteers to read aloud this passage, each volunteer reading one paragraph.

After the reading, divide participants into smaller groups of 3-4 members each. Explain:
- In your group, identify all the consequences of Abraham and Sarah's lie.
- Then think of a similar contemporary situation, in which one person's lie to protect him- or herself causes grief for many people.

Give groups 5-10 minutes to complete their discussions, then regather and discuss:
- Why did Abraham lie?
  — What were the consequences of Abraham's lie for Abraham? What do you imagine he went through after Sarah was taken to Abimelech?
  — What do you imagine Sarah went through, sent away from home to be with Abimelech?
  — What were the consequences for Abilmelech? for his wife? for his slave girls?
- Share your group's contemporary version of the story from Genesis.
  — What is the initial lie?
  — Who suffers because of the lie?
  — What does it take to "undo" the lie's damage?

4. Attitude Adjustment: WEB-O'-DECEIT

Ask group members to sit together on the floor in the center of the meeting space. Loosely tie one end of the string around your waist. Hold the string in your hands as you explain:
- I'll ask a question of the group.
- I'll then pass the string to someone. That person answers the question—lying, of course—wraps the string around him- or herself, passes the string to another member of the group and asks that person the same question.
- That person then answers the question, again with a lie, wraps the string and passes it on with the question.
- We will continue until everyone has answered the question at least once.
- The more outlandish your lie, the better.

Ask a question you think will yield the most creative "lies," for example:
- Why did you tell your last lie?
- Why didn't you study for that test at school?

When all group members have had the opportunity to give at least one answer to the question, observe that the entire group is bound together by a "web of deceit," spun by their own lies. Bring out the scissors and identify them as the "scissors of truth." Ask group members to cut themselves free of the string, *offering a truthful statement each time they cut through the string.*

5. Attitude Exit: PLEDGE

Ask group members to stand in a circle. Discuss:
- To what extent is lying a habit?
- How do we get ourselves out of the habit of lying?

After group members have made several suggestions, close the session by inviting members to pledge to cut down on lying. Offer each group member an opportunity to complete this pledge/prayer:
- Dear God, who only says the truth in love, this week I pledge to tell the truth when...

a division of Church Publishing Incorporated

600 GRANT ST., #400
DENVER, CO 80203
1.800.824.1813

LYING

ATTITUDE
FOR TEENS BY TEENS

EASY TO GAIN, HARD TO KEEP
by Jerry Berg

We all have relationships with others—friends, family members, spouses, co-workers, classmates, etc. What provides the foundation for relationships? Most are based on *trust*.

Trust is an interesting commodity—moderately easy to gain, hard to keep...and even harder to regain. In relationships, we allow people further into our lives; we trust them.

One of the chief assassins of trust is lying. Lying destroys trust. Breaking trust hurts the person who trusted.

Lying is a habit, a *bad* one, like scab-picking. We lie because it seems like an easy alternative to the pain of the truth, but how many more lies will have to be told to cover the first? With each lie, trust dies away. And with trust go integrity, self-respect and respect for others.

Personally, I sometimes do lie. Sometimes it seems like the only way to avoid disaster. Wouldn't you rather lie than really hurt someone by telling the truth?

In any case, you must decide for yourself. Always strive for integrity—the inner sense that you are consistently doing what you believe is right. Integrity is one of those things that is yours and nobody can take it from you. You can only lose it for yourself. Keep your integrity, have respect for everyone and don't take trust lightly.

Do you lie?

LIES *by Rachel Gluckstern*

Lies, lies, lies—she was sick of them. Her parents always used to say to tell the truth, for finding out they had been lied to would make things worse. That's how she felt too.

Why did people have to lie to her?

She didn't know where to go, who to turn to. Trust is a fragile thing, delicate to build but easy to destroy. Her trust had always been stronger than others, but now she could no longer turn a blind eye and a deaf ear, for the constant battery had caused her trust to finally shatter. Now she sat alone wondering how she could pick up the pieces of her life and whether or not she should even attempt to salvage the shards of her trust too.

Her parents: "We will always love you and stick by you no matter what."

Her friends: "We love you and will always be there for you."

Her boyfriend: "I love you and I'll never leave you."

But they had all lied, and now she was alone. Her boyfriend was out of state, maybe never returning. Her closest friends had abandoned her,

(continued on page 2)

Tell the truth.

© Copyright 2000
Living the Good News
a division of Church Publishing Incorporated
600 Grant Street
Suite 400
Denver, CO 80203
1 (800) 824-1813

Graphic Design & Illustration:
Carolyn Klass

TRUTH AND LIE INVENTORY

For each of the statements below, put a F in the blank if you believe the statement is false, put a T in the blank if you believe the statement is true.

___ I never lie.

___ I rarely lie.

___ I lie, but I feel bad about it afterwards.

___ I lie to protect myself.

___ I lie to protect others.

___ I lie to family members, but not to friends.

___ Sometimes it's okay to lie.

___ It's never okay to lie.

___ Everyone lies.

___ I know at least one person who never lies.

___ Jesus never lied.

___ Even Jesus lied from time to time.

___ There are sometimes good reasons for lying.

___ God wants us to always tell the truth.

___ God knows that an occasional lie is necessary.

___ Telling the truth always brings positive results.

___ Telling the truth is a way of trusting God.

___ I feel better about myself when I am honest, even if it causes trouble.

LIES (continued from page 1)

betraying things she'd shared in confidence. Her parents had withdrawn their love when she'd gotten into trouble, treating her with total coldness, acting like she didn't exist.

All the lying had left her to carry on by herself. This solitary existence felt like a punishment for daring to believe and trust in the others, for falling for the lies of others...

THE INSIDE STORY

GENESIS 20

[ ]

It's just a fib, a white lie, a slight misrepresentation, a misleading impression, that's all. Let's not quibble about details. You misunderstood. It's a trivial thing, a minor deception for your own good.

Check out Abraham in today's story. You may call it a political maneuver, a creative strategy, an act of self-defense or temporary insanity. Abraham calls it a half-truth, since Sarah was his half-sister. Clever, but not good enough. God calls it like it is: a lie.

We do the same thing, waffling around the truth. At times the truth can be beautiful and nurturing; at other times it can be strategically disastrous, unlovely and painful. But the truth is never anything but the truth, and a lie is never anything but a lie.

Like Abimelech's question in today's story, we ask: "Why do we do it?"

Look at Abraham's response. First, he had the impression that no one in the land feared God and that therefore they would have no qualms about killing him to get Sarah. Reason #1. We lie because we're afraid.

Second, he reasoned that the pagan's lack of reverence for God would lead to sin, but he overlooked his own lack of reverence for God that also led to sin. Reason #2. We lie because we forget God.

Third, he figured that a partial truth was good enough. Reason #3. We lie because we do not understand the nature of truth, which is a priceless whole that has no value in pieces.

Fourth, when Abraham remembered that "God sent him," and that God had a purpose for him, he concluded that the end justified the means. If Abimelech murdered him, it would thwart God's will, right? Reason #4. We lie because we want to control events according to our own understanding.

Four good reasons that only deceive us.

LEADERS' GUIDE

FOCUS

Ethics: Cheating

SCRIPTURE

Genesis 27:1–28:10

SCAN

Today's meeting examines cheating:
- Attitude Check encourages group members to cheat at a board game.
- Attitude Question explores cheating and its consequences.
- In Attitude Search, small groups lead each other in an exploration of an Old Testament story about cheating.
- Attitude Adjustment asks the small groups to think of and roleplay subtle forms of cheating.
- In Attitude Exit, group members suggest ways to overcome cheating and pledge to do less cheating.

STUFF

Bibles
photocopies of today's paper (pp. 81-82), 1 per participant
pens or pencils
chalkboard and chalk or newsprint and marker
familiar games, 1 per every 4 group members, for example, Monopoly®, Life®, Uno®, Yahtzee®, Chinese checkers, pachisi, etc.

1. Attitude Check:
DON'T GET CAUGHT

Welcome group members and invite them to choose and set up games to play. Arrange to have 3-4 players for each game.

Before beginning the games, explain:
- We have one new rule for our games

today: *Cheating is not only allowed, it's expected.*
- But as in a regular game, if you're *caught* cheating, you're out of the game.

Play the games for 15-20 minutes. Whoever is ahead (and still in the game) at that point is the winner for each game.

As group members help to put away the games, invite them to share their reactions:
- How many of us cheated at the game we were playing?
  — How did you feel, cheating?
  — What did you gain from cheating?
  — Was it easy or difficult to cheat? Explain.
- How many of us got *caught* cheating?
  — How did we feel when we got caught?
- Who among us chose *not* to cheat? Why?
  — How did you feel *not* cheating?
  — What did you gain from not cheating?
- How many of us who won think we won because we cheated?

2. Attitude Question: UNDER-STANDING CHEATING

Ask group members to sit together in a circle. Discuss:
- Define *cheating*.
- Why do people cheat? What do cheaters hope to gain?
- Think of our schools:
  — How widespread is cheating on homework, papers or tests at school?
  — What motivates students to cheat?
  — Who are the victims of cheating at school? Who loses out?
- Think of the adults you know:
  — In what ways do adults cheat?
  — What motivates adults to cheat?

— How widespread do you think cheating is in business? in government? in neighborhoods?
— Who are the victims of cheating in business? in government? in our neighborhoods?
● Describe a situation in which you were cheated.
— How did you feel?
— How did you handle it?
— What was the result?
● Describe a situation in which you cheated someone.
— How did you feel?
— How did the other person feel?
— What was the result?
● What do we risk by *not* cheating? In what ways does honesty pay off?
● Let's examine a biblical example of cheating.

3. Attitude Search: GENESIS 27:1–28:10

Distribute pens or pencils and copies of today's ATTITUDE paper. Divide participants into smaller groups of 3-4 members each. Ask groups to complete the activity Do Cheaters Prosper?, printed in the papers.

After about 15-20 minutes, regather the group and invite the small groups, in the proper order, to present their summaries of today's scripture story.

After the story has been summarized, ask the small groups, again in the proper order, to lead the larger group in a discussion of the story, using the questions prepared in their small-group discussions.

After all groups have had an opportunity to lead the discussion, ask:
● What have we learned about cheating from the story of Jacob and Esau?

4. Attitude Adjustment: MANY FACES OF CHEATING

Invite participants to return to the small groups of today's Attitude Search. Explain to groups:

● It's easy to identify cheating at games and cheating on tests as cheating.
● But there are many, subtler ways in which people cheat as well.
● With your group, brainstorm some of life's less obvious ways to cheat. Then prepare two or more quick roleplays that illustrate those ways to cheat.
● When we regather in a few minutes, you'll be asked to present your roleplays to the larger group.

Give groups about 10 minutes to discuss and prepare their roleplays. If necessary, offer these examples of cheating to groups:
● An athlete using steroids.
● A food manufacturer using inferior or spoiled ingredients.
● A restaurant serving smaller portions than pictured on the menu.

When groups are ready, invite each group to present its roleplays. After *each* roleplay, discuss:
● Who was cheating and how in this roleplay?
● Do you agree that this was cheating? Why or why not?
● What was the result of cheating in this roleplay? What further results could have been shown?
● What would have been the result if no one had cheated?

5. Attitude Exit: PLEDGE

Invite group members to stand together in a circle. Title chalkboard or newsprint *Overcoming Cheating*. Ask a volunteer to record group members' answers to this question:
● What advice can we give to someone caught in the cycle of cheating?

After group members have suggested a variety of ideas, close the session by inviting them to pledge to cut down on cheating. Offer each group member an opportunity to complete this pledge/prayer:
● Dear God of fairness and grace, this week I pledge not to cheat when...

a division of
Church Publishing
Incorporated

600 Grant St., #400
Denver, CO 80203
1.800.824.1813

CHEATING

ATTITUDE
FOR TEENS BY TEENS

CHEATERS *NEVER WIN?*

by Rachel Gluckstern

Have you heard the saying, "Winners never cheat and cheaters never win"? It's not completely true. I know; I've been the banker when playing Monopoly...and I *won*.

When you cheat, however, you lose the trust of others. Eventually you'll have no friends because none of them trusts you.

There are many ways to cheat: copying answers on a test, breaking a promise, sneaking into games, betting on something you have rigged, etc. All are dishonest. All lead to being distrusted and disliked.

Cheating can become a bad habit, so just like any other bad habit, you need to find ways to break it:

- One option is to go cold turkey—simply quit altogether. If you're in the cheating habit, resolve to stop it, completely, now.

- If you cheat at games or when placing bets, it might help to adopt an attitude of win some, lose some. Losing really is no big deal. Losing doesn't make you any less important or likable. A game's just a game. A little cash is just a little cash. And when you do win honestly, it's much more fun and satisfying because the win is earned.

- Do you cheat on tests and homework? Then try studying. You may be amazed to find it's actually easier to study than to find a place to

(continued on page 2)

CHEATED *by Jerry Berg*

New acquaintances, they sat side-by-side in a dimly lit jazz club. Bob's hand tapped the scarred table top as he listened to the jazz. Sean drank coffee and talked about his life. The conversation wound around like the hazy trail of smoke from the sputtering candle in the center of the table.

"What's in the suitcase?" Sean asked.

Bob slid the case to the table, popped the latches and brought out a beautiful chainsaw. Sean gasped: The saw was oiled and polished; the teeth gleamed in the light like flames from a torch. He held it, felt the incredible lightness. All of his life he'd dreamed of a chainsaw this wonderful.

Black thoughts crept into Sean's head. "How about a game of poker?" he asked. "If you win, I give you $500.00. If I win, I get the saw." Sean pulled a deck of cards from his pocket. "What do you say?"

They played.

And, as expected, Sean won: his four aces beat Bob's four queens. Bob handed over the chainsaw and smiled as Sean left, taking another slow sip from his coffee.

Sean raced to the forest, found a nice tree to cut down, yanked the starter cord and gripped the trigger in eager anticipation. Nothing happened. He frowned. The motor didn't turn over, not even once. He yanked again, then again. Nothing.

Sean popped the cover off the engine compartment..but there was no engine! Instead he found a clear, plastic reservoir filled with fluid.

Sean was angry, and he raced back to the club. "What's this?" he said, dropping the chainsaw to the table. Bob peeled the top off another plastic cup of cream and poured it into a fresh cup of java. He leaned forward and blew out the candle still struggling in the center of the table. The tip of the wick glowed orange. Bob picked up the chainsaw, clicked the trigger twice, and a small yellow flame flickered at the end of the saw. He used the flame to relight the candle.

He drank some more coffee, but said nothing.

Sean stared, first at the flame dancing on the candle, then at Bob's blank, uncaring face, then at the cards on the table—his cards—his special cards that had been left behind in his eagerness to try the new saw.

(continued on page 2)

© Copyright 2000
Living the Good News
a division of Church Publishing Incorporated
600 Grant Street
Suite 400
Denver, CO 80203
1 (800) 824-1813

Graphic Design & Illustration:
Carolyn Klass

ATTITUDE

DO CHEATERS PROSPER?

The story of Jacob and Esau is a story of family deceit, hatred, betrayal and grief...the stuff on which soap operas and talk shows thrive!

Your group has been assigned one part of today's reading from Genesis. Whatever portion of the story you've been assigned, here's what to do:

- First, read your portion of the passage together in your group.
- Second, summarize your portion of the story. Be ready to tell that part of the story to the regathered group.
- Third, write at least three discussion questions based on your portion of the passage. Your group will lead the larger group in a discussion using these questions. As you think of questions, keep these things in mind:
  — Don't ask questions that can be answered yes or no. Ask open-ended questions instead, questions that require extended answers.
  — Ask questions that uncover what you believe is important in the passage.
  — Ask questions that get at the idea of "cheating."

Use this space to record your ideas and questions.

CHEATERS *NEVER WIN?*

(continued from page 1)

hide your cheat sheet. Your mind is an amazing organ, capable of storing large amounts of information. Enjoy using it.

Now for one more saying: "If you cheat, you only cheat yourself." Completely true. Don't cheat your-self, it's not worth it.

THE _____

INSIDE STORY

GENESIS 27:1–28:10

Cheating. It's become so commonplace that it's practically expected. Surveys of students from high school through college show that the majority of them cheat frequently. When asked, students justify their behavior by pointing to the billionaire businessmen and women who have gained their fortunes by cheating. It's the way it's done, isn't it?

Sometimes we soften the word: bamboozle, gyp, swindle, fleece, dupe, bilk. These words imply that the victim (parent, sibling, teacher, employer, government) was a fool anyway, and it's his or her own fault.

We even admire clever cheaters: the one who can falsify a time card, who can get into the professor's computer system, who can get into the theater without paying, who can outfox the IRS, who can convince a parent that he or she made the curfew. It's creative planning, right?

You might think so upon first glance at today's story. Jacob is oh so smart, Esau is a dunderhead (it's his own fault), and Isaac is a sucker. Jacob simply took advantage of the opportunity that presented itself and, by the way, achieved God's purposes in the long run. Right?

Hardly. God's will could easily have been brought about without Jacob's cheating. The idea that God relies on our sin is ludicrous.

The outcome of Jacob's choices? Jacob was exiled for 20 years. He never saw his mother again. He was repeatedly duped, in turn, by his father-in-law, who first cheated Jacob out of the woman he loved and then cheated him of his wages. And finally Jacob was cheated (by his own children) out of his beloved son, Joseph.

There are two facts about cheating: 1) Cheating breeds cheating. Cheat once, and you'll feel forced to cheat again. Cheat on your homework assignments, and you'll need to cheat on your exams. 2) What you sow, you will reap. If you cheat, you will one day become the victim, the dupe, the fool. Just like Jacob.

CHEATED *(continued from page 4)*

Odd thing was, the solitaire game Bob had been playing had turned up more then four aces...six were showing...and Sean knew there were others. He had been caught. He stormed out of the club.

Bob sat smiling, drinking his coffee, sucking up the music through his ears and thinking about how he might market his new chainsaw lighters.

LEADERS' GUIDE

FOCUS

Ethics: Stealing

SCRIPTURE

Ephesians 4:28

SCAN

Today's meeting examines stealing:
- In Attitude Check, group members play a game that allows "stealing" of others' treats.
- Attitude Question explores the motivation behind and consequences of stealing.
- In Attitude Search, members expand on Paul's advice about stealing.
- Attitude Adjustment invites members to brainstorm the many subtle ways we can steal from God, others, ourselves and creation.
- In Attitude Exit, members pledge to do less "stealing" and more "giving."

STUFF

Bibles
photocopies of today's paper (pp. 85-86), 1 per participant
pens or pencils
chalkboard and chalk or newsprint and marker
a variety of edible treats, 1 per participant, for example, fruit, cookies, candy, pastries, etc. (**Note**: *Variety is the key; be certain to gather a different kind of treat for each participant. Having two or three particularly desirable treats will add interest to the activity.*)
slips of paper numbered consecutively, beginning with the number 1, 1 slip per participant
bowl or basket
4 large sheets of newsprint or butcher paper
colored felt markers
tape or tacks

1. Attitude Check: STOLEN TREATS

Display the assortment of treats in the center of the meeting space. Mix the numbered slips in the bowl or basket. Ask each group member to draw one numbered slip. Seat members in a circle around the displayed treats.

After all groups members have arrived and drawn slips, explain:
- Let's play a game that results in everyone getting one of the treats you see before us.
- Who is number 1? You're first. You get to choose one treat. You may retrieve it, but don't eat it yet. *(Let number 1 pick a treat.)*
- Who is number 2? You may either choose a treat from among what's left or steal the treat already chosen by number 1. *(Let number 2 choose or "steal" his or her treat.)*
- Who is number 3? You're next. You may either choose a treat from what's left or steal the treat from number 1 *or* number 2...

Continue for all numbers and players.
Note:
- Any given treat may be "stolen" as often as desired.
- Anyone whose treat is "stolen" immediately chooses a replacement treat from those yet unchosen (but may not steal an already chosen treat).
- Nobody eats a treat until the game is over.

When all treats have been chosen or "stolen," let group members eat their treats as they discuss:
- Who ended up with what they wanted?
- Who had something that they really wanted to have "stolen"? How did that feel?
- How did you feel as you "stole" something that someone else had chosen?

2. Attitude Question: BUT, HONESTLY...

Distribute pens or pencils and copies of today's ATTITUDE paper. Invite group members individually to complete the activity An Honest Look at Stealing, printed in the papers.

When members have finished, regather and invite volunteers to share their answers and insights, starting with all responses written in box 1, then the responses written in box 2, etc.

3. Attitude Search: EPHESIANS 4:28

Distribute Bibles and invite group members to turn together to Ephesians 4:28. Ask a volunteer to read this verse aloud. Discuss:
● When it comes to stealing, Paul (the author of this letter) says, "Stop!"
● But Paul doesn't leave it at that. He mentions three *positive* things to do instead. What are they?
● Think back to the things people stole from us, as we wrote in our papers. If those who stole from us could instead have done something positive for us, what might they have done?
● Think back to the different things we stole from others, also identified in our papers. If we replaced those items with something positive done for those from whom we stole, what would we do?

4. Attitude Adjustment: THE SUBTLETIES OF STEALING

Tape or tack four sheets of newsprint or butcher paper to the walls of the meeting space. Write the word *others* in large letters on the first sheet, the word *God* on the second, the word *myself* on the third and

the word *creation* on the fourth. Make available the colored felt markers. Explain:
● Move around the room, stopping at each sheet to write or draw at least one way in which you can steal from the person or thing listed on the sheet.
● Try to think beyond the obvious, for example:
— We can steal from our parents by robbing them of peace of mind.
— We can steal from God by undermining the effectiveness of a church service.
— We can steal from creation by polluting a stream.
— We can steal from ourselves by destroying our options for a future career.

Give group members 10-15 minutes to add to these sheets, then review what has been written or drawn and discuss:
● Which ways of stealing had you not thought of before?
● Which ways of stealing would you most want to avoid? Why?

5. Attitude Exit: PLEDGE

Write the title *From Taking to Giving* on chalkboard or newsprint. Ask a volunteer to record group members' answers to these questions beneath the title on chalkboard or newsprint:
● In what ways can we stop the many ways, obvious or subtle, that we take from others?
● In what ways can we be more open to finding ways to give and support others?

Close the session by inviting group members to pledge to cut down on the ways, both subtle and obvious, that they may be stealing. Offer each group member an opportunity to complete this pledge/prayer:
● Dear God, who is the God of generous giving, this week I pledge not to take from others when...

a division of
Church Publishing
Incorporated

600 GRANT ST., #400
DENVER, CO 80203
1.800.824.1813

STEALING

ATTITUDE
BY TEENS
FOR TEENS

JEANNIE by Jerry Berg

purse. One day, it occurred to Jeannie that it would be very easy to sneak an extra dollar. The dollar went unnoticed, so the next month she tried a couple of dollars. Taking extra became a regular thing. No one knew; no one cared. It was easy.

In high school, Jeannie got a job at a fast-food place. Before long, she worked the register, handling cash for much of her shift...and incidentally skimming off several dollars each night before closing out the register.

Eventually the manager got suspicious and started watching her

(continued on page 2)

Does Jeannie need the money? No, not really. All her needs are met, and then some: nice home, nice clothes, transportation when she needs it, and extra cash if she really wants something special.

So why does she steal?

It started years ago. Her parents gave her a good allowance. For several years, it seemed like a lot of money to Jeannie, and it was sufficient to get candy or toys—whatever she really wanted. Her parents trusted her, so much so, that when they were busy, her mom told her to go get her allowance out of her

---

#1 RULE: DON'T BE A CREEP
by Nate Fandel

Stealing?

You steal, and you hurt yourself.

You steal, and you defy God.

What do you gain from stealing? Material possessions. Are they worth becoming a crummy human being for?

Stealing has its perks, you say?

- Stealing stuff costs *nothing!* (Except for your self-respect and personal morality. And the eventual payback, since what goes around comes around.)

- Stealing can be *fun!* (Yeah, fun...the thrill of hurting someone else. Yippee.)

- Stealing is okay as long as you take *from the wealthy!* (If you were wealthy, and everyone stole from you, you and your employees would all be out on the street.)

- Stealing is okay because *everyone does it!* (Yes, and everyone dies, so I guess death's okay with you, too?)

Stealing leads to other unhealthy stuff. Comfortable with stealing? What's the next step? What else can you do to hurt others and not feel bad about it?

Stealing? Take a good, long look at your life and decide: Is this really the direction I want to go?

ATTITUDE

© Copyright 2000
Living the Good News
a division of Church Publishing Incorporated
600 Grant Street
Suite 400
Denver, CO 80203
1 (800) 824-1813

Graphic Design & Illustration:
Carolyn Klass

AN HONEST LOOK AT STEALING

In this blank, describe things that people have stolen from you. Remember to think broadly...people can steal not only tangible objects, like money, CDs or clothes, but also intangibles like self-respect, peace of mind or relationships.

In this blank, describe a time when you stole from someone else. What did you steal? Why did you do it?

In this blank, describe how you reacted when someone stole from you. How did you feel? What did you think about? How did you handle it?

In this blank, describe the effect your stealing had on the other person. Describe the effect stealing had on you.

JEANNIE (continued from page 1)

closely. Jeannie got caught. She ended up waiting for her parents at the police station.

"No big deal," she thought. "All I've done is lose a job."

But it was more than that.

No one else wanted to hire her.

And no one in her family trusted her. New rules and stricter curfews dropped like rain around her.

"All this for a few dollars? It's not fair!" she would say to her friends, as they rechecked and held tighter to their wallets.

EPHESIANS 4:28

THE INSIDE STORY

There are as many reasons to steal as there are things to steal. Laziness, peer pressure, greed, jealousy, insecurity, fear, anger. There is always a reason whenever there's an opportunity.

The best reason seems to be that it just doesn't matter. After all, it's mostly minor things: an employer's supplies, a tube of lipstick, a bag of Skittles, a pair of jeans. It's not like it really hurts anyone, is it? Business owners factor shoplifting into their prices, right?

But that pair of earrings slipped into the purse, that video carried under a coat, that box of computer paper loaded into your own car—they do matter. Stealing is one of the Big Ten (commandments, that is), right after murder and adultery, and right before lying and coveting.

Stealing is part of that old self "that was being destroyed by its deceitful desires." It's destructive. It eats away your innards, and leads to moral rot.

In today's verse, Paul describes the cure. It's not enough to shake the finger and say no, no. We're not children any more. It's not enough to grit the teeth and decide to be theft-free. A more potent cure is prescribed.

A preacher earlier this century told the old Greek myth of Ulysses's temptation by the luring and fatal songs of half-human creatures. Ulysses tried to plug his ears so that he could resist their enchantment. Orpheus, on the other hand, did not worry about the songs' deadly charm. Instead of plugging his ears, he simply sang a song so much more beautiful, more powerful, more piercing that the songs of the creatures were like screeching and squalling.

Paul understands this well. The secret to overcoming any temptation is to replace it with a more dynamic desire. Those who steal must stop stealing and turn their creative energies to earning enough to share with those in need.

Followers of Christ who give up stealing and take up generosity, responsibility and hard work sing a powerful song.

LEADER'S GUIDE

FOCUS

Growing Up: Becoming an Adult

SCRIPTURE

Luke 2:41-52

SCAN

In today's meeting, group members explore the nature of maturity:
● Attitude Check asks group members to imagine their adult selves coping with problems.
● In Attitude Question, members create a Road to Maturity that illustrates growing up.
● Attitude Search tells the story of one of Jesus' significant growing-up moments.
● In Attitude Adjustment, group members suggest ways to clear the way to maturity.
● In Attitude Exit, members respond to today's meeting from both a child's and an adult's viewpoint.

STUFF

Bibles
photocopies of today's paper (pp. 89-90), 1 per participant
long, narrow strip of butcher paper or newsprint
colored felt markers
tape or tacks
pins
construction paper

1. Attitude Check:
MY FUTURE SELF

Invite group members to sit in a circle. Ask a volunteer to respond to the following:
● It's 25 years in the future. You are the parent of two teenagers, ages 14 and 16, who refuse to join you on the family vacation this summer. You feel hurt and angry. *How will your adult self handle this situation?*

Give the volunteer 2 minutes to respond, then repeat the exercise with other volunteers and other situations. Use the following situations or add others of your own:
● It's 20 years in the future. You've made a huge mistake at the restaurant you manage: You were to deposit the day's receipts at the bank, but you left the bag in the dining room. Now it's gone. *How will your adult self handle this situation?*
● It's 30 years from now. You falsely accused your teenage son of using the car without permission and damaging it. Now you discover that the car was hit when parked in front of your house. *How will your adult self handle this situation?*

Discuss:
● In what ways do we imagine that our grownup selves will differ from our current selves?

2. Attitude Question:
ROAD TO MATURITY

Tape or tack one end of a long strip of butcher paper or newsprint halfway up one wall of the meeting space. Let the paper run down the wall and across the floor, ending up running halfway up the wall on the opposite side of the room.

Write the title *BIRTH* at the beginning of the paper and the title *MATURITY* at the other end. Discuss:
● You see before you the Road to Maturity.
● Define the word *maturity*. What does it mean to be at the maturity end of this road?
● Maturity seems to be a matter of degree. Some people are more mature

ATTITUDE FOR TEENS BY TEENS

than others; possibly no one ever becomes completely mature. At what age do *most* people achieve *some degree* of maturity? *(When group members have reached consensus, ask a volunteer to write this age at the end of the road.)*

Invite two or three volunteers to place themselves on the paper at the approximate point of their current ages. *(If, for example, group members agree that 30 is the age of maturity, a 15-year-old volunteer would stand in the middle.)* Ask these volunteers:
● Are you closer now to birth or maturity?
● As you look forward to maturity, what obstacles to maturity still lie ahead?

Invite responses to this final question from all group members. Members could suggest obstacles such as *an abusive parent* or *lack of direction.* As each obstacle is named, ask a new volunteer to create a sign out of construction paper that identifies that obstacle and place it at the appropriate place on the Road to Maturity.

3. Attitude Search:
LUKE 2:41-52

Distribute Bibles. Explain that today's scripture tells the story of an important "growing-up" point in Jesus' life. Recruit three volunteers to read Luke 2:41-52 aloud, one taking the part of *the narrator,* one the part of *Jesus' parents* (in v. 48) and one the part of *Jesus* (in v. 49).

Invite group members to participate in a "reverse quiz." Instead of asking questions, you will give the answers and it will be the group's responsibility to supply the questions. Allow for a variety of responses after each of the following "answers":
● *Answer:* a deepened sense of God's purpose for him
● *Answer:* worried, angry, puzzled, confused and maybe a bit unnerved
● *Answer:* physical strength, mental ability and especially knowledge of God's will and the human heart

Now distribute pens or pencils and copies of today's ATTITUDE paper. Invite group

members to write several "answers" of their own, following the directions in the activity Reverse Quiz, printed in the papers.

When group members have finished, ask them to offer their "answers" to the group and invite the group to ask possible "questions" for each "answer." Conclude:
● What steps toward maturity does Jesus take in today's story?

4. Attitude Adjustment:
CLEARING THE WAY

Invite group members to return to the Road to Maturity. Start walking from the "birth" end of the road. Each time you encounter an *obstacle*, follow this procedure:
● Ask a volunteer to assume the role of the obstacle. The *obstacle* identifies him- or herself and explains how he or she keeps travelers from maturity.
● The travelers discuss and propose realistic ways to overcome the *obstacle.*
● The *obstacle* removes and destroys the sign of the obstacle he or she represented and joins the travelers as they continue on the road.

Repeat this process for all *obstacles.* When all *obstacles* have been cleared and the group has reached "maturity," discuss:
● To what extent is "maturity" a choice?
● In what ways do we "learn" maturity?
● What do you think helps us mature faster, life's successes or life's failures? Explain.
● In what ways can a relationship with God contribute to maturity?

5. Attitude Exit:
MAKING CHOICES

Invite each group member to offer a childish response to the meeting; for example:
● I wanted to be an *obstacle* and instead I just stood on the stupid road.

Invite each group member to offer adult responses to the meeting; for example:
● I learned that failure helps me mature.

a division of
Church Publishing
Incorporated

600 GRANT ST., #400
DENVER, CO 80203
1.800.824.1813

BECOMING AN ADULT

ATTITUDE

FOR TEENS BY TEENS

WHEN WILL I GROW UP?

by Nate Fandel

I sit in the back of the store under the bright fluorescent light, behind the cheap, 70's, green and brown desk and think to myself, Why did I do this again? I should have learned from last week. When will I grow up?

It happened about like last time. I entered the store in uniform—the red shirt and black pants characteristic of this particular supermarket. Once inside, I pinned on my name badge.

I stock for a few minutes and then call a few price checks. I'm doing a fine job, as usual.

Just then the manager walked up to me. "How long have you worked here, son? And how come I've never seen you before?" The voice of authority.

It all comes out pretty quickly: I don't work here, and, in fact, I've never been employed in my life. I picked this store randomly to work at today, the uniform the result of a quick trip to the local Goodwill.

I do this every once in a while... something stupid, I mean. Can't I help it? I wish I would get my act together and control myself. Maybe when I'm an adult I'll understand these things and get some self-control.

Meanwhile, the manager sits across the desk and asks, "What is your problem?"

I think to myself, Blah, what a bunch of... Hmm, what am I going to do after I leave? I probably ought not to tell him my real name. I've got to meet some friends at four...

And then, When will I grow up?

WHAT'S AHEAD by Rachel Gluckstern

What do you hope to get out of life? Do you want money? kids? Do you want to be a scientist? a singer? Do your friends want the same things you do?

Growing up is something that will happen to you sooner or later. It might be time to start thinking about what you want out of life. I know what I want; I want to be a writer or an actress. I want to marry and have kids. I want to feel happy. These are *my* goals, so they may not be yours.

My goals come from my values, and my values differ a lot from others, and that's okay.

That's something to think about: *your values.* What are yours, and how will they benefit you in the future? What morals and principles do you believe in and uphold? It's important to be able to stick by what you believe.

As you grow older, you will realize that people have different beliefs than you do. Incredibly enough, it's all right! Honest! People can have different views and wants than you and still be okay! I suggest not trying to force your ideas on anyone, as I'm willing to bet big money that you hate it when people force things on you.

(continued on page 2)

ATTITUDE

Living The Good News

REVERSE QUIZ

Your group just thought of several "questions" to match the "answers" shared by your leader. Think of an additional "answer" or two for the group, based on the reading from Luke 2:41-52. It's okay if your "answers" have several possible "questions."

Use the space below. Be ready to offer your "answers" to the group when you regather.

WHAT'S AHEAD
(continued from page 1)

What do you want from life? Think about it long and hard. There's only one way to get what you want —*go out and get it*. Don't wait around for something to come to you, because it never will. Waiting

doesn't produce anything, it just wastes time.

Life has much to offer; it holds so much variety. My advice? Appreciate difference. Grab onto life with both hands.

THE INSIDE STORY

Luke 2:41-52

Kids—both little and big—like to dream about what they're going to be when they grow up. Perhaps they wonder, with some dread, if they're going to end up as bone-brained as some of the adults they know. Good Lord, spare us! There is good news: If you ready yourself, you can move into adulthood prepared to live it fully, intelligently, vigorously.

In Jesus' time, a thirteen-year-old boy would enter the community as a man. When Jesus was twelve, he was on the threshold of adulthood; he took this transition seriously and prepared for it.

The story begins with Jesus' submission. Mary and Joseph head for Jerusalem to celebrate an important feast. Jesus goes along. He accepts the significance of that event. Do we take advantage of the spiritual leadership that is offered us? Do we engage ourselves in the life of the community? Or are we too busy with our own agendas?

Maturity includes submission, but it also involves separation. See Jesus linger behind though his parents head home? His parents are shocked and hurt. But Jesus knows that it is time—time for him to move into a new place of relationship to God. Are we ready to seek God's way and will for us? ready to venture out of childhood security and beyond our parents' expectations? Or do we shrink before the enormity of God's love and call?

Then Jesus submits again, understanding his need for more time. He returns home in obedience, yielding to parental authority. Do we see clearly our undeveloped places? Or are we too impatient, too headstrong to welcome good counsel?

"Jesus grew both in body and in wisdom, gaining favor with God and men."

LEADER'S GUIDE

FOCUS

Growing Up: Life Goals

SCRIPTURE

Matthew 5:1-20

SCAN

In today's meeting, group members identify and discuss life goals:
● Attitude Check asks group members to rank goals for the future.
● Attitude Question compares and contrasts members' goals.
● In Attitude Search, members sculpt life goals suggested by Jesus in his Sermon on the Mount.
● Attitude Adjustment gives members an opportunity to "balance" their life goals.
● Group members complete two statements about life goals in today's Attitude Exit.

STUFF

Bibles
photocopies of today's paper (pp. 93-94), 1 per group member
pens or pencils
chalkboard and chalk or newsprint and marker
modeling clay
sculpting tools

1. Attitude Check: IDENTIFYING GOALS

Welcome group members and distribute pens or pencils and copies of today's ATTITUDE paper. Invite group members to complete the activity Future Goals, printed in the papers.

While group members complete their charts, number chalkboard or newsprint 1-11.

When members have finished, summarize the ratings on their charts by adding up everyone's assigned points, item by item, and writing them on chalkboard or newsprint after the appropriate numbers.

Circle the items with the five highest scores and ask:
● Which goals ranked highest?
● Let's examine these goals.

2. Attitude Question: UNDERSTANDING GOALS

Keep the chart completed in today's Attitude Check in view of all group members. Discuss:
● Look at the chart that you completed in your paper:
— This chart reflects what you believe will be your goals when you are an adult. How do these goals differ from your goals *now*? Explain the difference.
— Note your top three goals. Why did you give these goals the highest ranking?
— In what ways are your top three goals reflected in your life today?
— What goals did we write in space #12? How many of these goals do we share in common? How are these goals reflected in our lives today?
● Look at our summary chart on chalkboard (newsprint):
— What surprises you about these rankings? Which did you expect?
— How do you imagine these rankings would compare to those of our parents? our grandparents? our teachers at school? other members of our parish?
— Imagine that Jesus had completed this chart for himself. How might he have distributed his 25 points?

ATTITUDE FOR TEENS BY TEENS

— Would we want our distribution of points to look like Jesus'? Why or why not?

3. Attitude Search: MATTHEW 5:1-20

Distribute Bibles and modeling clay. Divide participants into three groups. Assign each group one portion of today's scripture, divided as follows:
● Matthew 5:1-12
● Matthew 5:13-16
● Matthew 5:17-20

Explain to groups:
● In your group, read aloud your portion of today's scripture.
● Identify the life goals Jesus is suggesting in your verses. What goals does Jesus say we are to have in life?
● Either individually or together as a group, use modeling clay to sculpt these goals. Your sculptures can be either literal or symbolic; for example, the goal of "being salt for the world" could be shown by a sculpture of an open, speaking mouth.
● Be ready to show and explain your sculptures to the larger group.

Give small groups time to complete their reading, discussion and sculptures, then gather and invite participants to show and explain their sculptures, starting the presentation of each sculpture with the statement:
● Here's another goal Jesus sets for us...

When all sculptures have been presented, discuss:
● How are Jesus' goals for us similar to the goals on our chart on chalkboard (newsprint)? How are they different?

4. Attitude Adjustment: BALANCING GOALS

Invite participants to return to the small groups of Attitude Search. Ask groups to discuss the following questions (perhaps copied on chalkboard or newsprint so they can be seen by all groups):
● How do we know when we have the proper mix of goals in our lives? How do we know when our goals are "in balance"? "out of balance"?
● What part does God play in helping us sort out our future goals?

Gather participants and ask:
● After today's discussion, how would you rearrange the points as you distributed them in the chart in your paper?

Give group members time to look again at their charts in their papers, making any change they might wish to make. After several minutes, invite volunteers to share their changes with the group. Discuss:
● What can we do to help us balance our current goals?
● What can we do *now* to help us balance our *future* goals?

5. Attitude Exit: CIRCLE RESPONSE

Invite group members to stand together in a circle. Explain:
● As we grow and change, so do our goals. This will always be the case.
● Our goals aren't what they were, and they aren't what they will be.

Invite volunteers to complete this statement:
● One change I've seen in my goals is...

When all who wish to complete the statement have done so, invite volunteers to complete this second statement:
● One change I expect in my goals is...

Conclude by praying:
● Dear God, let all our goals be grounded in you, our source of power, love and compassion. *Amen.*

For the next meeting, ask group members to consider:
● What might my future goals contribute to the world?

a division of
Church Publishing
Incorporated

600 GRANT ST., #400
DENVER, CO 80203
1.800.824.1813

LIFE GOALS

ATTITUDE
FOR TEENS / BY TEENS

subjects are like and what you could do in those areas.

- Enlist the help of a school counselor. A counselor can help you plan your schedule to give you broad exposure to lots of future possibilities.
- Set realistic goals and strive for them. Don't expect to be the next Michael Jordan if you're a third stringer on your basketball team. On the other hand, challenge yourself to try for what you might not otherwise have done.
- Be there; be present; do it; play.
- Get all you can from your education.

The best advice for your future? Be the best you can in whatever you try.

CAREER by Jerry Berg

The world is large and filled with lots of choices. And, unfortunately, many of the choices seriously affect the rest of your life.

What will you do after high school? Will you get a job? Will you go to college? Now's the time to start asking, "What do I *want?*"

Here's some help:

- Make a list of the things you enjoy doing. Name a job that fits each item on your list.
- Make a list of the skills you have. Name a job that fits each item on this list, too.
- Take a wide range of classes in school. Find out what different

---

MY FATHER by Nate Fandel

My father:
a successful V.I.P. of an oil corporation and its subsidiaries
got the money he's coveted his whole life
lives in a nice house
doesn't beat us
harmonious American home
money to buy unnecessary, environmentally incorrect products

My father:
unhappy person who hates his job
commutes to work over three hours each day
leaves in the morning before the sun comes up
gets home after dark
day after day after day
until summer when we go on summer vacation
and he still works day after day after day
all-too-frequent business trips to Texas, D.C., etc.

comes home with time to sleep and eat
off to work again

My family:
only consistent activity we have is he and I go out to coffee on Saturday mornings
doesn't involve my mother
doesn't include my thirteen-year-old brother
don't have much family structure at all
see each other in passing
we *do* have a family—that's good—more than many
but I'd trade the money for some real family structure
for just one meal a week with all four of us
that won't happen now with my mother in school getting her master's
and the family saving for college for my brother and myself

My life:
important decision...
people and happiness are more important than money
millionaire?
rather a happily starving artist who spends time with people who love me

© Copyright 2000
Living the Good News
a division of Church Publishing Incorporated
600 Grant Street
Suite 400
Denver, CO 80203
1 (800) 824-1813

Graphic Design & Illustration:
Carolyn Klass

ATTITUDE

Living the Good News

FUTURE GOALS

What goals do you have for adulthood?

You have 25 points to divide among the items in the chart below:

- Give more points to goals you value highly.
- Give fewer points to goals you value a little.
- Give no points to goals you don't care about.

Make sure your total points add up to 25—no more, no less!

Whatever I do with in life, these are my goals...

1 to enjoy adventure and risk: ____ points	**2** to be physically active: ____ points	**3** to help the environ- ment: ____ points
4 to have fun and laugh a lot: ____ points	**5** to be wealthy: ____ points	**6** to be challenged mentally: ____ points
7 to have a good marriage: ____ points	**8** to know and love God: ____ points	**9** to have meaningful friendships: ____ points
10 to feel satisfied and content: ____ points	**11** to feel secure and safe: ____ points	**12** *other:* _____ ____ points

Be ready to share your results with the group.

INSIDE STORY

MATTHEW 5:1-20

As Christians, the most important thing is *not* what we believe and *not* what we do. The most important thing is who we are. Christianity is an identity. So when we think about our goals in life, our priorities, our agendas, we begin by understanding that *we are Christians*, which means that whatever we do or say or think is done or said or thought in the spirit of Christ.

> Christianity is an identity...which means that whatever we do or say or think is done or said or thought in the spirit of Christ.

Look at the Sermon on the Mount. Here Jesus sums up this spirit with the word "righteousness." "Righteousness" simply means a relationship with God where you and God are in sync, in harmony, in agreement about everything.

The Beatitudes offer an eight-step approach to that kind of relationship. *Spiritual poverty*—knowing that you are just a clay jar, nothing unless you are filled with God. *Mourning*—grieving over the sin that keeps you from being filled, that destroys creation, that murders children, that wrecks your family. *Humility*—bringing your pain to God and submitting to God's ways in hope.

Hungering for God's will—letting the desire for God's power and love take over every part of your life. *Mercy*—seeing God's tender love meet your desperate needs and extending it to others. *Purity*—ruthlessly cutting out of your life everything that blocks God's love or resists God's ways.

Peace—working fiercely to free others from those things that block God's love or resist God's ways. *Persecution*—realizing that enjoying this kind of relationship is like driving the wrong way on a one-way street; others will curse you for it.

Such a relationship is like salt and light in a tasteless and dark world.

LEADER'S GUIDE

FOCUS

Growing Up: Making a Difference

SCRIPTURE

Luke 16:19-31

SCAN

Today's meeting invites group members to dream of the difference they, as adults, will make in the world:

- In Attitude Check, group members create their own tombstones, complete with epitaphs.
- Attitude Question explores the ways in which members influence others.
- In Attitude Search, members discuss Jesus' parable about missed opportunities that could have made a difference.
- Attitude Adjustment gives group members 15 minutes to make a difference.
- In Attitude Exit, members silently commit to making a difference in the world, both now and in the future.

STUFF

Bibles
photocopies of today's paper (pp. 97-98), 1 per group member
large sheet of butcher paper or newsprint
colored felt markers
colored construction paper
scissors
tape or tacks

Before the meeting cover one wall of the meeting space with butcher paper or newsprint. Title the paper *They Made a Difference*. This paper will provide the background for the "graveyard" mural created in today's Attitude Check. You might wish to draw a few details on the mural, for example, a few trees, a fence, a church in the background, etc.

1. Attitude Check: GRAVEYARD

Welcome group members and make available the construction paper, scissors and markers. Distribute today's ATTITUDE paper. Explain:

- Imagine it is now decades into the future. We've all grown up, lived full lives, made a difference in the world...*and died.*
- Create the tombstone that will stand at the head of your grave.
- On your tombstone, write an epitaph for yourself. You'll find suggestions for writing epitaphs, along with examples, in your papers.

Let group members construct their tombstones of construction paper. As they finish, invite them to tape or tack their tombstones to the graveyard mural prepared **before the meeting**. Invite members who finish first to add other drawings to the mural. When all tombstones have been added to the mural, invite each group member to read aloud his or her tombstone.

2. Attitude Question: CHANGE THE WORLD

Ask group members to gather around the "graveyard." Discuss:

- What does our graveyard tell us about our future hopes? our expectations of ourselves as adults?
- In what ways do we hope to change the world?
- Each day, for better or worse, each one of us influences other people.
  — Whom do you influence now? For example, in what ways do you influence your family members? friends? younger kids you know?
  — Who influences you? in what ways?
  — Whom do you hope to influence in your adult life?

ATTITUDE FOR TEENS BY TEENS

- Jesus made a huge difference, not only in his society, but also in the world during the past 2,000 years:
  — In what ways did Jesus leave his mark on the world?
  — From what you know of Jesus' life, to what extent did he "go with the flow"? To what extent did he "fight to make a difference"?
- How important is it to "leave a mark" in the world? What other options are there?
  — What's to be risked by letting life happen around you without trying to change things? What's to be gained by this approach?
  — What's to be risked by trying to "leave your mark"? What's to be gained?
- Let's see what Jesus says about making a difference.

3. Attitude Search:
LUKE 16:19-31

Distribute Bibles and recruit three volunteers to read aloud Luke 16:19-31, the first taking the part of *Jesus (the narrator),* the second the part of *the rich man* and the third the part of *Father Abraham.* Discuss:
- While he was alive, what opportunities did the rich man miss for making a difference in Lazarus's life?
- What message does the rich man want Lazarus to bring to his brothers?
- What opportunities for making a difference in someone's life will we have in our meeting today? at home this evening? at school this week?
- What message about making a difference do you think the rich man would want us to hear?
- What message about God could we bring to people this week that would make a difference in their lives?

4. Attitude Adjustment:
MAKE A DIFFERENCE *NOW!*

Divide participants into small groups of 3-4 members each. Explain to groups:
- Your group has the next 15 minutes to make a difference in the world.

- You may make that difference here in our meeting room, somewhere else in the building, outside on the street—*anywhere and with anyone.* Just be back here to tell us about it in 15 minutes.

When all groups have returned after 15 minutes, discuss:
- Tell us how your group made a difference.
- How do you feel about the difference you made?
- What other "15-minute projects" could we have undertaken?
- What greater impact could our groups have had if they had been given an hour to make a difference? 24 hours? a month? a year?
- What motivates people to make a difference in the world?
  — What motivated Jesus to make a difference?
  — To what extent can Jesus' motivation also be ours?

5. Attitude Exit:
SILENT MEDITATION

Ask group members to stand together in a circle. Invite them to close their eyes for a final meditation. Say, slowly and thoughtfully:
- In the silence of your own heart, complete this prayer: God, help me to make a difference in the world by... *(Pause.)*

Conclude by praying:
- God of action, God of change, God who makes a difference, as we grow, help us to turn the world upside with your love and power. *Amen.*

Note: Today's meeting offers a good opportunity to discuss with group members the possibility of starting a group service project. What community needs has your church identified? How could group members meet one such need? Could group members participate in a project already underway? Bring today's future-oriented discussion into the present by encouraging concrete, immediate service to others.

*a division of
Church Publishing
Incorporated*

600 GRANT ST., #400
DENVER, CO 80203
1.800.824.1813

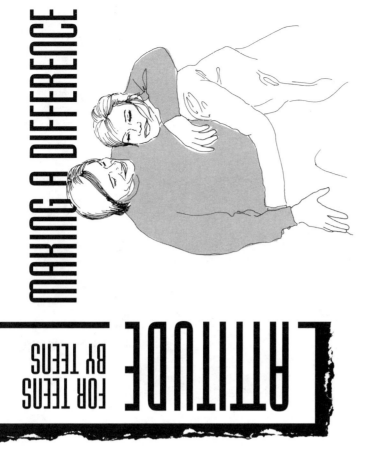

MAKING A DIFFERENCE

INDIVIDUALITY: RISKS OR REWARDS by Rachel Gluckstern

"Oh it's *her*! I can't believe the way she acts! Why can't she be like everyone else?"

Individuality is hard to develop, especially as a teenager. We all want to be accepted, so we often hide who we are to gain that acceptance. We all fear that if we are ourselves, we won't be liked.

So we put on appearances to blend in. We try hard to be "average." We go with the flow, because it's easy. No one calls us weird, and, since everyone shares our opinion, we never have to stand up for something hardly anyone believes in. We can go through life with average grades, neutral opinions and an average

depth of friendship. Life holds fewer problems for those who choose to be average.

But who remembers average people? Who remembers people who go with the flow?

The people we remember are the ones who stand against the flow. Yes, you might get shot down for doing so, but if you succeed, you reap big rewards. You leave your mark and make a difference.

Look at Ghandi, Martin Luther King, Rosa Parks and Jesus. They proclaimed loud and clear what their

(continued on page 2)

MAKING A DIFFERENCE by Jerry Berg

Has an adult you've known made a difference? What has that person done that matters? Will people remember him or her after he or she is gone?

These questions may seem of little or no consequence now, but one day you'll ask these questions about yourself. Then they'll seem a lot more important. Have *I* made a difference? How will *I* leave *my* mark in the world? Will people remember *me* when I'm gone?

I often think of my own dream. Everybody wants to leave behind a sort of legacy, such as a cure for the common cold. I want to write a play. Not just any play, I want to write a science-fiction play. It's said that

through writing, one achieves immortality. The words live on. Decades from now—maybe even centuries—I want people to be transformed by my words. I want to be known around the world for my play. That's my dream.

Everyone must have a dream. The fewer dreams and goals a person has, the closer they are to death. All great women and men have had dreams. Find your dream, your goal, and make it a reality for the world. Imagination, creativity and knowledge gain worth when they become tangible through our actions. By these actions you will judged; by these actions you will be remembered.

ATTITUDE

WRITING YOUR EPITAPH

Gregori Jones
1978-2028
Here Lies Greg
Who Lost a Leg
Saving the Life
Of His Child and Wife

Mariah Delgado
1975-1996
Her deep love
for others
will live beyond
her brief years.

Elizabeth Riggleman
1963-2042
First Female
President
of the United States
of America

An epitaph is a short statement, in verse or prose, that honors someone who has died. It usually mentions who the person was or what he or she did.

Write an epitaph on your "tombstone." Let your epitaph reflect what you expect to be remembered for after you die.

INDIVIDUALITY: RISKS OR REWARDS? (continued from page 1)

opinions were, and tried to make a difference in the world. They faced obstacles. Many people hated them. They imprisoned Ghandi. They assassinated Martin Luther King. They arrested Rosa Parks. They crucified Jesus.

Should these people just have kept to themselves? They tried to bring about better things for the world that never could have come about without them. Imagine what it would be like if Rosa Parks had moved on the bus when told to, if Martin Luther King had tried to use violence—or not tried at all—to end segregation, if Ghandi had never tried to find peace between countries and religions, if Jesus had never

preached or had refused to go to the cross...

No one expects you to be like these people, but trying to be yourself with your own ideas will make a difference. Going with the flow can be better for your health, but going against it can bring you greater happiness and rewards. If you are stifling yourself, let it out! If you still watch Sesame Street, be proud of it! If you hate Fritos, admit it! If you are for gun control, stand by it! Swimming with the waves is easy; swimming against them takes courage and strength.

Nothing ventured, nothing gained.

THE INSIDE STORY

LUKE 16:19-31

Come meet Lazarus. No? I'm not surprised. We want to *avoid* Lazarus. His infected acne oozes pus. He smells. The flies crawl on his lips and nose. An unpleasant character, you say? You flinch at the sight of him? Then take a look at *this* man: meet *Dives*.

Now Dives (which is Latin for "rich man") is the kind of person we most want to schmooze with. He smells good; he looks good; he's business-wise and savvy about all the latest trends.

Now, see Dives's mansion? Look closely there at the electric, guarded gate. There? Do you see? It's Lazarus, lying in the bushes. Now look, here comes Dives's chauffeured limousine. Dives looks out, sees Lazarus and turns away in disgust. Lazarus's broken body doesn't move, and neither does Dives's stone-cold heart.

Dives is thrilled when Lazarus finally dies. Good riddance, he thinks. He was an eyesore.

Dives's family is thrilled when Dives dies. The money is theirs. And there, on the other side, Lazarus revels in the comforts of Paradise while Dives writhes in the torments of Hell.

Today Lazarus sits at the gate of our youth, the doorway of our amusements and security and dreams, longing for just a scrap. Maybe he's our brother who is struggling with his weight; maybe he's our mom who feels overwhelmed by the family's demands; maybe it's the girl at school who is the butt of everyone's jokes.

Lazarus doesn't make much noise and he really doesn't pester us much, but neither does he get up and move on. He's just there. An unyielding but silent opportunity to open our hearts to the pain of others.

LEADER'S GUIDE

FOCUS

Growing Up: Aging

SCRIPTURE

Luke 2:21-38

SCAN

Today's meeting explores the nature of aging as a part of the growing-up process:

- In Attitude Check, senior guests give a brief talk about growing old.
- Attitude Question provides an open forum for group members to ask questions of the elderly.
- Group members discuss the story of two prophetic elders important in the life of Jesus in Attitude Search.
- A guest leads group members in a game in Attitude Adjustment.
- In Attitude Exit, guests and group members exchange a blessing.

STUFF

Bibles
photocopies of today's paper (pp. 101-102), 1 per group member
colored construction paper
colored felt markers
scissors
pins

Before the meeting invite two or more elderly members of your parish to join your group for today's discussion. Ask these guests to prepare a few remarks about aging, for example:

- What has surprised you about aging?
- What are the special benefits of age? special challenges?

In addition, invite one or more of the guests to prepare to lead the group in a game in today's Attitude Adjustment. Urge this guest to pick a group game common to their teenage years.

1. Attitude Check: GUESTS

Welcome both group members and special guests (see **before the meeting** note). Make available construction paper and markers and ask all participants to create name tags for themselves that include two or three small drawings that reflect their special interests.

Then go around the circle introducing yourselves, explaining the drawings on the tags.

Ask the senior guests to share their observations about aging, prepared beforehand. After the talk, thank the guests and continue with Attitude Question.

2. Attitude Question: BUT WHAT ABOUT...?

Open the meeting for questions. Invite group members to ask any question of the guests. Here are sample questions suggested by the teenage writers of ATTITUDE:

- Was it a shock to grow old?
- When did you notice you were older?
- How do you regard your teenage years? Do they seem far away or close? How relevant to your life do they seem now?
- How is the world different from when you were a teen?
- Do you like the life you've led? Do you like the life you're leading now?
- How important is your faith to you? How has your relationship to God changed as you've aged?
- What are the toughest lessons you've learned in life?
- How have your values changed as you've grown?
- How have families changed over the years?
- What physical changes have come from aging? How have you dealt with these?

3. Attitude Search:
LUKE 2:22-38

Distribute Bibles and invite group members to turn to Luke 2. Ask a volunteer to read aloud verses 21-35. Discuss:
● This passage tells of an important "growing up" event in Jesus' life. Why is he in Jerusalem with his parents? (See vv. 22-24.)
● What clues in this passage suggest that Simeon is an older man?
● In your own words, what does Simeon predict about Jesus? (See vv. 29-33 and 34-35.) What will Jesus do? Who will Jesus be?
● In what ways do Simeon's words about Jesus come true?

Ask a volunteer to read aloud verses 36-38. Discuss:
● Who is Anna?
● In your own words, what does Anna predict about Jesus? According to Anna, what will Jesus do?
● In what ways do Anna's words about Jesus come true?
● In our church, what "prophetic words" do the elderly bring? How do our elderly parish members, like Simeon and Anna, help us to understand who Jesus is? what God asks of us? how much God loves us? what part we play in God's plan?
● In our church, how can we make sure we hear our "Simeons" and "Annas"?

4. Attitude Adjustment:
TEACH US

After the potentially heavy discussion of today's first three activities, group members and guests take part in a guest-led game.

Ask the senior guest who prepared **before the meeting** to lead the group in a game. Here are two classic possibilities:
● *20 Questions*:
Choose an *It*. *It* thinks of the name of a famous person. Group members ask *It* questions, one at a time, in an effort to guess the name chosen by *It*. Group

members may only ask questions that can be answered with Yes or No.

Members use their questions to narrow the options. Typical early questions include:
— Is this person living?
— Is this person real?
— Is this person female?

A maximum of 20 questions may be asked. If someone correctly guesses the name, that person becomes the new *It*. If the name remains unguessed after 20 questions, *It* shares the name and picks a new name for another round of play.

● *Telephone*:
Ask group members and guests to sit in a large circle. The leader chooses a statement to whisper in the ear of the person to his or her left. That person whispers the same phrase—as he or she heard it—into the ear of the next person in the circle. In this manner, the statement gets passed completely around the circle.

No person may repeat the statement in the ear of his or her neighbor, even if the neighbor had trouble understanding. *Each person repeats what he or she thinks was heard.*

The last person in the circle says aloud the statement he or she heard, often with hilarious results, since the statement will evolve as it's passed.

5. Attitude Exit:
BLESSING AND PRAYER

Invite the senior guests to stand in the middle of the group circle. Distribute today's papers and gather around the guests, placing hands on the guests' heads and shoulders. Repeat the blessing printed in the papers.

Switch roles, asking group members to stand together in a tight circle as the senior guests stand around them and repeat the same blessing.

a division of Church Publishing Incorporated

600 GRANT ST., #400
DENVER, CO 80203
1.800.824.1813

AGING

A CONTEMPLATION by Rachel Gluckstern

He could feel it—the change happening. He was growing up. Getting older, changing.

Age...what a weird word it was to him. It was a noun, an adjective, a verb. It could describe someone or something or stand for a period of time. *Age, aging, aged, to age.*

He had never really thought about it before, what it would be like to be old. Oh sure, he had joked about it and made fun of old people, but he had never really understood. Teenagers always try to grow up, so they can get on with their life, but right now he wanted to grow *down.*

Old age was beyond his comprehension. It was hard to imagine *adulthood*. What exactly was it, anyway?

When are people truly adults?

He thought he'd be a teenager forever, but in actuality, people are only teenagers for six years. The end of his teenage years was drawing near.

What would he be like in five years? Would those go by like the last five? What would he be in ten years? in thirty? Thirty years seemed *(continued on page 2)*

ATTITUDE

FOR TEENS
BY TEENS

AN INTERVIEW WITH MABEL BOGGS
by Rachel Gluckstern

Note: Mrs. Boggs was a teenager 60 years ago, in the 1930s.

Rachel: What did you learn as a teenager that helps you out today?

Mrs. Boggs: I grew up during the Depression, so I learned how to be careful with money. I learned how to have fun without money. My friends and I had strong religious beliefs and high morals regarding sex and alcohol, and things like those. We knew how to have fun without those things.

Rachel: Did your belief in God help you as a teen?

Mrs. Boggs: Yes. My friends and I were all very religious, and my father was a minister. I believe that the beliefs we had helped us sustain our morals. There were probably people who had lower standards, but none of them were my friends.

Rachel: Did you enjoy growing up?

Mrs. Boggs: Yes, even though it was the Depression, and I was poor—we *all* were poor—I found it fun to be a teenager. I went to college and nursing school and became a registered nurse. My parents were both educated and they passed on the importance of education to my brother and me. I was involved with sports and plays, and my family was very close. I enjoyed being with them.

Rachel: What advice do you have for teens today?

Mrs. Boggs: I would say be careful of who you pick as your friends and who you get involved with.

© Copyright 2000
Living the Good News
a division of Church Publishing Incorporated
600 Grant Street
Suite 400
Denver, CO 80203
1 (800) 824-1813

Graphic Design & Illustration:
Carolyn Klass

ATTITUDE

BLESSING

Loving and protective God,
grant these your children
strength to meet life's challenges,
opportunities to share their wisdom,
and delight in the world's beauty.

Amen.

A CONTEMPLATION (continued from page 1)

like so much time, yet he'd only be in his forties. Middle-age really, but it sounded so old.

What would happen in thirty years? Would he be happy? successful? rich? fat? married divorced widowed father childless...the thoughts flowed together...the possibilities endless.

And what would he be like in *fifty* years? Half-a-century from now placed him in his sixties. What would he be like in his sixties? his

seventies? So much time; *so little time.* Death could hit anytime, he might not make it to seventy.

When does a person truly become old?

He laughed, but he was scared, because he didn't know what age would bring. He couldn't imagine liking different music, losing hair, having a family. Most of all, he couldn't imagine being old.

When would he be...old?

THE [INSIDE STORY]

LUKE 2:21-38

Name the elderly in your life. No, no, not your parents. I know they *seem* old, but they're not. Think of the ones who move slowly, who can't quite hear what you say, who peer over the steering wheel and drive in the middle of the road, who grocery shop once a week and buy only one bag of groceries. Now you get the picture?

Now think of Mary. She was about your age when she gave birth to Jesus. No doubt, she felt all the confusion and anxiety about her future that any young person (or old person, for that matter) feels. You'd think that what Mary needs is another young mother to encourage her.

But Luke tells us that, when Mary brings the Baby to the temple, she runs into an old man and an old woman, two unlikely voices of comfort and guidance in Mary's bewildering world.

Simeon is a man of prayer and keen spiritual desire, a man who moves with the Holy Spirit. Anna is a prophet who spends all her time worshiping, fasting and praying. These are focused people. They're not distracted by all the hype of youth; they're not burdened with all the anxieties of peers and careers. They can *see*, really see. And they have a word for Mary.

Simeon and Anna were old, and their age made them even more available to God. Their wisdom, their long faithfulness and their inner harmony with God prepared them to encourage young Mary in unique ways.

Who are the old people in your life? Are you as open to them as Mary was? What do they see when they look at you? Listen...

When Mary brings the Baby to the temple, she runs into an old man and an old woman, two unlikely voices of comfort and guidance.

LEADER'S GUIDE

FOCUS

Growing Close to God:
Reading the Bible

SCRIPTURE

Matthew 4:1-11

SCAN

Today's meeting introduces the first of
four ways to draw closer to God—
spending time reading the Bible:

- In Attitude Check, teams of group
  members play a game of Bible trivia.
- Attitude Question explores knowledge
  of and attitudes toward scripture.
- In Attitude Search, members model
  Jesus' skillful use of scripture.
- Attitude Adjustment invites members
  to find something personally meaning-
  ful in the Bible.
- Attitude Exit challenges group mem-
  bers to spend time reading their
  Bibles this week.

STUFF

Bibles
photocopies of today's paper (pp. 105-
  106), 1 per participant
cardboard or old file folder
felt markers
masking tape

Before the meeting do *one* of the following for the game in Attitude Check:

- Locate a room that has a floor made
  up of distinguishable tiles. Label a
  game path using these tiles, marking
  both a "start" and an "end" tile. You
  will need a path of at least 20 spaces.
- Create a game path in your usual
  meeting space by taping to the floor
  at least 20 sheets of cardboard or old
  file folders. Mark the first space "start"
  and the final space "end."

Add interest to the game by including
"special" spaces along the path, for example:

- Return to start.
- You may choose to answer an extra,
  bonus question. Correct? Move ahead
  two. Incorrect? Go back five.
- Skip your next turn.

1. Attitude Check: BIBLE TRIVIA

Welcome group members and explain
that today's meeting begins with a game
of Bible Trivia. Distribute Bibles and divide participants into two teams. Ask
each team to pick one member of their
team to be that team's *playing piece.*

To play the game:

- Alternate asking questions of teams
  (*not* individuals).
- Team members may confer before
  giving answers.
- If a team answers correctly, their *playing piece* moves one space along the
  path.
- If a team answers incorrectly, the
  playing piece remains where he or
  she is.

Here are sample questions. Add others.
You could also invite members of the
opposing team to suggest questions for
their opponents:

- What's the first book of the Bible?
- How many books are in the Bible?
- Who was swallowed by a big fish?
- Who was sold into slavery by his jeal-
  ous brothers?
- Name five of the 10 commandments.
- What man did Jesus' mother marry?
- How many disciples did Jesus have?
- How did John the Baptist die?
- What was the Apostle Paul's original
  name?

The winning team is the team whose
playing piece reaches the *end* space
first.

ATTITUDE FOR TEENS BY TEENS

2. Attitude Question:
WHY READ THE BIBLE?

Begin by exploring some basic Bible facts. As you lead this discussion, help all group members to feel okay about what they do or do not know about the Bible. *Questions:*
● What is the Bible?
● What's the difference between the Old and New Testaments?
● What authors contributed to the Bible? In what sense is God the "author" of the Bible?
● When were the various parts of the Bible written?
● How do you find your way around the Bible?
  — Name the different Bible books.
  — How are the Bible books arranged?
  — What are *chapters? verses?* How do they help us find our way in the Bible?

Shift the discussion from an examination of Bible *facts* to the *meaning* of scripture:
● Why do people read the Bible? What does the Bible offer us?
● For those of us who regularly read our Bibles, how does it fit with our day-to-day lives? What does the Bible have to do with our friendships? our life at school? our families?
● Respond to this statement: *The Bible is the owner's manual for life.*

3. Attitude Search:
MATTHEW 4:1-11

Divide participants into smaller groups of 3-4 members each. Explain:
● In your group, read Matthew 4:1-11.
● After reading, discuss: How does Jesus use scripture in these verses?

Give groups 5-10 minutes, then regather and ask volunteers from each group to share their group's insights.

Ask groups to continue discussing:
● Look again at Matthew 4:1-11. In your group, retell the story in a contemporary setting.
  — Let Jesus be found in one of your schools.

— Let the temptations be three real temptations faced by students in your school.
— Let Jesus respond to each temptation using verses from the Bible. If you can't think of actual verses, respond with statements you believe reflect biblical truth.

Give groups time to come up with their new temptations and responses, then regather and ask groups to share at least one temptation and response each.

4. Attitude Adjustment:
BIBLE SURFING

Invite participants to return to the small groups of Attitude Search. Explain:
● In your small group, go Bible surfing.
● In Bible surfing, you open up your Bible and browse, looking for something helpful or meaningful for you.
● Bible surfing is one of many ways of getting into the Bible.
● If you're new to Bible surfing, try starting with the Psalms in the Old Testament or the Gospel of John in the New Testament.
● When you've found something, read it aloud and tell why you chose it.

5. Attitude Exit: CHALLENGE

Distribute copies of today's ATTITUDE paper. Invite group members to read silently the activity Challenge, printed in the papers.

Discuss:
● Does anyone already have a favorite verse from scripture? What is it and why is it a favorite?
● The teenage writers of ATTITUDE chose the four verses that appear in your paper because they had special meaning for them. What might each of these verses have meant to the writers?

Conclude today's meeting by praying:
● Dear God, help us to find you in the Bible this week. Draw closer to us as we seek to draw closer to you. *Amen.*

a division of
Church Publishing
Incorporated

600 GRANT ST., #400
DENVER, CO 80203
1.800.824.1813

READING THE BIBLE

ATTITUDE

FOR TEENS BY TEENS

DEFEND YOUR FAITH
by Jared Crain

There are many ways to grow closer to God. One is reading scripture. Many Christians read the Bible daily to learn both more *about* God and more *from* God. Daily Bible reading can fill you with hope and provide a better understanding of God's plans for us.

Well, it *could* fill you with hope and it *could* fill you with a better understanding of God's plans...if you have faith in it.

But if you *don't* have faith in it, then what? How can it strengthen you when there is so little proof that the things in the Bible actually happened? Christians often feel attacked when people say things like, "What proof is there that any of this exists anywhere but in your mind?" Complex debates over the historical validity of the Bible have started with just this question. Arguments range from the accuracy of atomic dating techniques to the amount of space dust there is on the moon. People carry a great deal of conviction for and against the Bible.

So how can Christians respond to these challenges? Some, when challenged, lose faith. Because they fear making big faith decisions with so little "proof," they drop the faith altogether.

Others, when challenged, acknowledge and affirm the role of faith in their lives. When they believe that God exists and loves them, they find great truth in the Bible. They *choose* to believe in God, and the Bible helps them. Faith in God's word (the Bible) follows as you have faith that God does exist and does love you and does want to lead you.

This faith is easily reaffirmed when you glance about and see your close friends in Christ, when you experience God in prayer, and when you see others who have given their lives to Christ and now give others a piece of God through service in Jesus' name.

So read your Bible. Approach it with the same confident belief with which you embrace God. You may be surprised when your faith proves itself.

DRIFTING AWAY
by Matt Sheen

I've been drifting away from God.

My relationship to God—it's just not what it used to be.

Before, with God, I always knew I had someone to depend on, someone who'd be there when things were bad.

Maybe that's when the problem started—things started going my way. It was easy to turn to God when I needed help. But then I got the lead in the school play. I worked up the nerve to ask out the girl who sat in front of me in English class. I made new friends and started going to parties. Things were working out. Finally I had a life!

But with lines to memorize, dates to go on and parties to attend there wasn't much time to set aside for God. I started missing church to make up the sleep lost on weekends.

And then, even when I did take the time to try to reconnect with God, it was hard to even talk to God. Too much time had gone by.

I want to regain what I have lost.

(continued on page 2)

© Copyright 2000
Living the Good News
a division of Church Publishing Incorporated
600 Grant Street
Suite 400
Denver, CO 80203
1 (800) 824-1813

Graphic Design & Illustration:
Carolyn Klass

ATTITUDE

Living the Good News

Each of the four meetings dealing with Growing Closer to God concludes with a personal challenge. This week, the writers of ATTITUDE challenge you to:

• Read your Bible for a few minutes a few days this week.

• As you read, look for one small section of scripture that is meaningful to you.

• Memorize that small section, whether it's a phrase, verse or passage. Be ready to share it in the next meeting.

Write your chosen section of scripture here:

The following verses are favorites of the teenagers who wrote this week's ATTITUDE. You could choose one of these if you can't find one of your own:

• Psalm 30:5a [God's] anger lasts only a moment, his goodness for a lifetime.

• Jeremiah 29:11 I alone know the plans I have for you, plans to bring you prosperity and not disaster, plans to bring about the future you hope for.

• Philippians 4:6 Don't worry about anything, but in all your prayers ask God for what you need, always asking him with a thankful heart.

DRIFTING AWAY (continued from page 1)

I glance over at my Bible, laying on the bookshelf, dusty with neglect. Maybe that's where I could begin.... Maybe a game of "Bible roulette"?

I take down the Bible and brush it off. I flip the pages rapidly and come to a sudden halt. Looking down I see Mark 12:30, "Love the Lord your God with all your heart, with all your soul, with all your mind, with all your strength."

Okay, God, I pray silently. That's the beginning.

MATTHEW 4:1-11

Jesus believed scripture to be the word of God: revealed, safeguarded, given.

So what's on your reading list? Is it a little out of control? How far behind are you in school reading? Any college catalogs sitting around? Several back issues of your favorite magazine? Another computer manual? The Bible?

What? The Bible? You've got to be kidding. Something written thousands of years ago (a little out of date, wouldn't you say?) about some very strange things (like what's the resurrection got to do with anything?) and some people who are long gone (will we ever really get quizzed about Gideon or Elijah or the third king of Judah?).

Yet, in today's story about Jesus being tempted by the devil, we see Jesus relying on just one thing: his knowledge of the Bible. He defended his relationship with God, resisted evil, found his way in a confusing situation and obeyed God by quoting scripture. Jesus believed scripture to be the word of God: revealed, safeguarded, given.

Yeah, but times are different now. We're told that the Bible is just a bunch of human opinions, not the word of God. Yet the odds of all those books of the Bible being written with such accuracy, defended with such passion and lived with such power over thousands of years is, well, rather like a bucket of paint being thrown at a canvas resulting in the Mona Lisa. But you decide.

Maybe you'll never have to defend your faith or resist evil or find your way in a confusing situation or obey God...and maybe you will. If so, there isn't another book out there that's going to give you what you need like the Bible will.

Jesus said, "The scripture says..." Do you know what the scripture says? Do you know the truth?

LEADER'S GUIDE

FOCUS

Growing Closer to God:
Fellowship

SCRIPTURE

Acts 2:42-47

SCAN

Today's meeting introduces the second of four ways to draw closer to God—fellowship with other believers:

- In Attitude Check, group members share the results of last meeting's challenge, then play a game that illustrates our need for others.
- In Attitude Question, members explore the nature of Christian community.
- Attitude Search looks at a scriptural example of Christian fellowship.
- The game in Attitude Adjustment demonstrates the power of fellowship.
- Attitude Exit challenges group members to fellowship with someone from the group in the coming week.

STUFF

Bibles
photocopies of today's paper (pp. 109-110), 1 per participant
chalkboard and chalk or newsprint and marker
pens or pencils
16 splints (3" x 24" pieces of wood or other flat, rigid material)
roll of gauze and scissors, 12" strips of bandage or shorts length of twine
4 paper cups
water
paper towels

1. Attitude Check: POINTS OF CONTACT

Before beginning today's game, invite

volunteers to share the result of last meeting's challenge:

- What verses or phrases did you find in the Bible during the last week?
- Which did you memorize?
- Why were these meaningful to you?

Clear the center of your meeting space and mark start and finish lines 25-30 feet apart. Multiply the number of members in the group by .6 and round up to the nearest whole number (e.g., 16 members x .6 = 9.6; round up to 10). Announce this number and explain that this number is the number of "points of contact" the group is allowed as they move together across the room from the start to the finish line. Explain:

- Only the announced number of points of contact may touch the floor.
- Everyone must move together as a connected unit.
- Switching points of contact once you've started is not allowed.
- Everyone must be connected.

Give the group time to choose their points of contact and attempt the move across the room.

2. Attitude Question: DEFINING FELLOWSHIP

Discuss the opening game:

- How did the members of the group help each other?
- What did you learn from each other?

Write the title *community* on chalkboard or newsprint. Discuss:

- Define *community*.
- What different communities (not specifically Christian) are we a part of?
- What does being in community do for us?

Add the title *fellowship* to chalkboard or newsprint. Discuss:

- Define *fellowship*.

ATTITUDE FOR TEENS BY TEENS

- What's the difference between community and fellowship?
  — What's different about *Christian* community?
  — What *Christian* communities are we a part of?
  — What different roles are there in these communities? What different roles do you take?
- How are you important in your church community? in *this* community (our group)?
- How does being in a Christian fellowship bring us closer to God?
- Let's look at a New Testament example of Christian community.

3. Attitude Search: ACTS 2:42-47

Distribute Bibles, pens or pencils and copies of today's ATTITUDE paper. Divide participants into smaller groups of 3-4 members each. Ask groups to complete the activity How Are We Doing?, printed in the papers.

While groups discuss, copy the chart found in the activity How Are We Doing? on chalkboard or newsprint.

When groups have completed the activity, regather and share the results of the discussions. Ask a volunteer to complete the chart on chalkboard or newsprint with the observations made by members of the small groups. Encourage discussion when members disagree.

4. Attitude Adjustment: FELLOWSHIP POWER

Recruit four volunteers. Using the boards and gauze or cloth strips, splint the arms of the volunteers so that they cannot bend their arms at the elbows.

Pair two of the volunteers. Hand each of the remaining two volunteers a paper cup filled with water. Explain to these solitary volunteers:

- Two things are true of you: One, you are dying of thirst; you have never been this thirsty in your life, and you would do anything for a drink of water. Two: you are alone; you have no one around to help you, no community, no fellowship.
- Unfortunately, you also have two broken arms, so it's going to be tough to get a drink.
- Try.

Let the solitary volunteers work alone to get a drink. Obviously, they cannot bend their arms to bring the cups to their mouths. Do not allow them to help each other, nor to get help from other group members. Eventually the solitary volunteers will either give up, spill the water or get wet as they attempt to pour the water into their mouths.

Turn to the paired volunteers. Hand each of them a paper cup of water. Explain:
- You too are very thirsty. You too have broken arms.
- But you also have each other.
- Take care of your thirst.

Obviously, these two volunteers can give each other water to drink. After they have done so, untie the splints and discuss:
- What does this exercise illustrate about the benefits of Christian fellowship?
- How does Christian fellowship help us to know God better?

5. Attitude Exit: CHALLENGE

Explain to group members:
- Last week you were challenged to know God better by spending time in the Bible.
- This week you're challenged to get to know God better by spending time in fellowship.
- Sometime this week, call one other person in this group and just talk with them for a few minutes. Consider choosing someone you don't know very well. Ask how the person is doing and what he or she has been going through.

To conclude the meeting, gather members in a circle. Move forward and embrace each other in a big, group hug.

a division of Church Publishing Incorporated

600 GRANT ST., #400
DENVER, CO 80203
1.800.824.1813

FELLOWSHIP

ATTITUDE
FOR TEENS BY TEENS

DEFINING FELLOWSHIP

by Jared Crain

We get a snapshot of the early Christian Church in Acts 2:42-47. There we learn that the four things most valued by the first believers were the gospel, the sacraments, prayer and *fellowship*.

Fellowship? Yes. Back then, the people of the Church "shared their belongings with one another..., according to what each one needed. They had their meals together in their homes, eating with glad and humble hearts..." These sentences from the book of Acts describe the acts of fellowship.

Why is fellowship important in a relationship with God? Fellowship allows Christians to gather in a safe environment where they can:

* worship God without fear of persecution
* discuss and affirm their values and beliefs
* learn how to take their faith and love out of the Church into a needy world

It is in this way—through daily fellowship—living out God's word with the support of fellow believers—that the message of Jesus spreads and helps others.

(continued on page 4)

1

GROWING CLOSER by Matt Skeen

John was a bit leery. What was he in for?

His family had moved into the area three weeks earlier. This morning, after church, a guy named Mike had introduced himself. Mike asked, "Why don't you come with me to youth group tonight?" John reluctantly agreed to go—after much persuasion.

At the last minute, John changed his mind. He tried to call Mike to tell him not to pick him up, but Mike had already left home. Now John waited for the doorbell to ring. Brrring. Time to go.

Two hours later, Mike dropped John back home. John was excited. Though he had started the evening tense and uneasy, barraged by all the new names he now couldn't remember and embarrassed by having to play some strange games, he eventually had felt part of the group. He enjoyed singing praises to God—something he would never have done on his own. The discussion introduced him to a number of new ideas. He found himself sharing his own thoughts with new friends. The group prayer was also a fresh experience for him; he felt God's presence in the room like never before.

Later that night, John sat on the edge of his bed, still thinking about his time with the youth group.

"God," he prayed aloud, "I think I've discovered a new way to grow closer to you."

DEFINING FELLOWSHIP

(continued from page 1)

In a fellowship based on the love and teachings of Jesus Christ, the qualities of a faithful Christian are nurtured and demonstrated. Only through loving God and showing others how to love God will we create a community that is strong enough to show the world the love, power and glory of God.

4

ATTITUDE

Living the Good News

HOW ARE WE DOING?

With the members of your small group, read aloud Acts 2:42-47.

When you've finished reading, rate the groups named across the top of the chart on each of the seven characteristics of Christian community listed down the left side of the chart. Rate them from 1 (definitely true of this group) to 6 (definitely *not* true of this group).

	My Church	My Christian Friends	This Group
1 "spending time learning" (v. 42)			
2 "sharing meals and prayers" (v. 42)			
3 "sharing miracles and wonders" (v. 43)			
4 "sharing belongings" (v. 44)			
5 "distributing money as needed" (v. 45)			
6 "meeting day after day" (v. 46)			
7 "praising God" (v. 47)			

Be ready to share the results of your discussion—summarized in your chart—when the group regathers.

THE INSIDE STORY

ACTS 2:42-47

"Being a Christian would be easy if it weren't for all the other Christians."

Have you ever muttered that to yourself after a particularly difficult time at youth group or in church? If you've been a Christian for long, you probably have.

There's nothing quite like a Christian with an attitude (whose opinions you don't share), who struggles with bad habits (that are definitely worse than yours) or who just plain drives you crazy to shake your faith up. It's easy to excuse the pagan jerk, but when the jerk's a Christian...well, how are we supposed to get along? Better question: *Why* are we supposed to get along? *Why* do we need each other?

Look at today's verses, which describe amazing Christian fellowship. Their relationships are centered on Christian teaching, worship and prayer; the people are characterized by hospitality, generosity and joy. They like to be together. And all this fellowship makes God glad. That's what the gospel is all about: bringing together God and us in a great embrace.

Our society makes fellowship difficult sometimes. It's easier to be alone: watching TV, working on a computer, driving a car, listening to a CD, playing with virtual reality. But it's when we're together, really with each other as believers who struggle with faith and obedience, who seek a deeper relationship with God, who long for the peace that only God provides, that we learn about the love of God which descends into our relationships and makes them powerful and profound. And there, together, we discover the love of God that takes such enormous pleasure in our camaraderie and affection and mutual support and servanthood.

Can't do that alone.

LEADER'S GUIDE

FOCUS

Growing Closer to God:
Prayer

SCRIPTURE

Matthew 26:36-46

SCAN

Today's meeting introduces the third of four ways to draw closer to God—prayer:

- In Attitude Check, group members experience a variety of new ways to pray.
- In Attitude Question, members discuss their beliefs about prayer.
- Attitude Search examines Jesus' prayer in the Garden of Gethsemane.
- Attitude Adjustment invites members to personally address Jesus.
- Attitude Exit challenges group members to spend time in prayer during the coming week.

STUFF

Bibles
photocopies of today's paper (pp. 113-114), 1 per participant
cardboard or old file folder
candle and candle holder
matches
see the **before the meeting** note for additional materials

Before the meeting set up six prayer stations around the room. At *each* station place:

- an index card on which you have copied that station's directions and
- the necessary materials, if any.

Here are the six stations:

- *Hymnal Prayer*
  — Directions: Find a hymn whose words are directed to God, for example, "Take My Life and Let It

Be." Silently read the words of the hymn as a personal prayer to God.
  — Materials: hymnals or songbooks
- *Psalm Prayer*
  — Directions: Look through the Psalms for a psalm that you like. You might check out Psalms 1, 23, 31, 51, 61 and 100. Read the psalm as a personal prayer to God.
  — Materials: Bibles
- *Sculpt a Prayer*
  — Directions: Use modeling clay to sculpt a prayer to God. You could fashion something that reflects a feeling you have for God, something for which you are thankful, etc.
  — Materials: modeling clay
- *Write a Prayer Poem or Story*
  — Directions: Write a brief poem or story to God. Let your poem or story say something about your gratitude to God, a request for God, something you don't understand about God, etc.
  — Materials: writing paper and pens
- *Draw a Prayer*
  — Directions: Use the available drawing materials to draw a prayer to God. You could draw something that reflects a feeling you have for God, something for which you are thankful, etc.
  — Materials: drawing paper and pastel crayons, colored chalk or colored pencils
- *Meditation*
  — Directions: Sit comfortably, close your eyes and imagine that God is sitting next to you. For a minute, just sit silently, knowing God is nearby. For the remaining time, talk to God in the silence of your own heart.
  — Materials: none

1. Attitude Check: PRAYER STATIONS

Welcome group members and explain:

- This week's meeting focuses on prayer.
- Around the room are six prayer stations. At each station you'll find directions for a way to pray.
- You'll have time to visit three of the six stations, with 5 minutes at each.

Let participants choose their first stations and let them begin. After 5 minutes, ask group members to switch to new stations. After members have finished their visit to their third station, gather and discuss:
- Who prayed in a new way?
- Which of the methods of "connecting with God" meant the most to you?

2. Attitude Question: WHY PRAY?

Invite group members to share their thoughts on prayer:
- What is prayer to you?
- In what different ways do you pray?
- What do you most often pray about?
- What is the purpose of prayer? What might prayer do for us? for God? for others?
- Many people have questions about prayer:
  — Some people wonder why we should pray if God knows everything already. How would you answer this question?
  — Some people have trouble believing that God really answers their prayers. What do you think? Does God listen? Does God answer? How do you cope with unanswered prayer?
  — What other questions do you have about prayer?
- Why do we often *not* pray? What are common obstacles to prayer?
- For you, when is a good *time* for prayer? Where is a good *place* for prayer?
- Let's look together at a powerful example of prayer from the Bible.

3. Attitude Search: MATTHEW 26:36-46

Distribute copies of today's ATTITUDE paper and Bibles. Divide participants into smaller groups of 4-5 members each. Ask groups to complete the activity A Painful Prayer, printed in the papers.

When groups have finished, regather and discuss:
- What did you learn about prayer from the story of Jesus in the garden?

4. Attitude Adjustment: ADDRESSING JESUS

Seat group members in a circle. Leave an empty chair somewhere in the circle. Light the candle and place it in the center of the circle. Dim the lights. Explain:
- I have lit this prayer candle for a soft, quieting focus for prayer.
- The empty chair in our circle represents Jesus. He is here with us, seated there, ready for us to speak to him.
- In a moment you'll have a chance to speak directly to Jesus. When you do, remember that prayer is simply speaking with a friend, someone who cares for you and wants to be with you.
- Prayer requires no special words or attitude—whoever we are *right now* is who Jesus wants to meet with. Whatever we're thinking or feeling is okay.

As group members quiet down, help them visualize Jesus sitting in the empty chair. You can make his presence real by directing a prayer to him, speaking to the empty chair; the more convincing you are at this point, the more powerful this prayer experience will be for group members. After you have prayed, invite volunteers to do the same.

5. Attitude Exit: CHALLENGE

Ask group members to stand in a circle. Invite prayer requests. When all who wish to share have done so, leave group members with this challenge:
- This week, talk to God. Whenever something important comes up, bring it right to God, right then and there.
- At other times this week, pray for the requests that people in our group have just shared with us.

a division of
Church Publishing
Incorporated

600 Grant St., #400
Denver, CO 80203
1.800.824.1813

PRAYER

ATTITUDE
BY TEENS FOR TEENS

THE HUM
by Lori VanDeman

I kneel here
and I feel pieces of the universe
coursing through my veins
power and beauty incarnate
flowing over the bridges
and through the loopholes
in my system
eyes shut tight to all
but the stars
colliding peacefully in my mind
deaf to all
but the hum of my own systems
the coursing of blood and water and oxygen
a pleasant sound like that
of an old fluorescent light
mmmmmmmmmmmmmmmmmmmmmmmm
or an aquarium
like the one in my room
when I was little
a sound so relaxing
that every muscle in my body
melted away at night in my sleep
those fish died
and the aquarium was sold
at a garage sale
but this hum does not die
it is not for sale
it is become a part of me
in my mind
yet by my side
a constant vibration of light
bringing me to
a peace everlasting
my mind contains more
than I have learned
and now it flows over
with a love
that transcends all understanding
"for those who believe
no explanation is necessary"
if you close your eyes at the sun
you see red
if you close your eyes in prayer
you see a pure white light
"for those who believe
no explanation is necessary"

GOD'S VOICE
by Jessica Kirk

Close your eyes. A Spirit has come over you. A prayerful Spirit. The Holy Spirit. Let this Being guide your thoughts and put forth from your lips new words. Set aside your memorized prayers for a minute and speak to God in your own private, spiritual language. Are you familiar with God's voice? Do you recognize God's touch? Soft and understanding. You know the one.

Have a cup of coffee and invite God into your heart; talk with God. Tell God how you are feeling and listen to what God has to tell you. Remember that a conversation has two voices, and that God is as excited to talk with you as you are to talk with God.

Prayer is personal and different for every individual. It takes on many forms—a song, a poem, a dance, a work of art—all can be prayers. God gave each of us unique gifts, and through these gifts we give back to God. Prayer—the use of these gifts—is the way you communicate and establish a relationship with God.

So when you feel the wind of the Spirit come upon you, be not afraid.

(continued on page 2)

ATTITUDE

Living the Good News

A PAINFUL PRAYER

With the members of your small group, read Matthew 26:36-46.

When you've finished reading, discuss:

- How is Jesus feeling as he struggles in prayer in the garden? How do you think he feels as he prays? when he discovers that the disciples are sleeping the first time? the second time? the third time?
- When have you felt like Jesus feels? When have you felt like grief? anguish? sorrowful? crushed? afraid? lonely?
- Describe Jesus' prayer in the garden.
- When have you prayed like this? What were you praying for?
- What was the outcome for Jesus of his prayers in the garden?
- What was the outcome for you when you prayed so strongly to God?

GOD'S VOICE (continued from page 1)

Instead, invite it to stay with you and inspire you. Let the Spirit join with you—become one with you— as you pray:

Let prayer be important in your life. It's the link between you and your Creator; choose to keep it strong.

Close your eyes. Say, "God, I love you." See what happens. You won't regret it.

THE INSIDE STORY

MATTHEW 26:36-46

In a world of science, high technology and power politics, prayer seems quite illogical. Think about it: You are in charge of your own destiny. You get rewarded for hard work and ingenuity. You get what you negotiate. Right?

Then what is it about prayer, reaching out to God with requests and thanks and confession and longing, that persists in a time of survival of the fittest? People still pray. Why?

Observe Jesus, who prepares for his execution with prayer. He feels the agony and fear that only humans can feel, that you, perhaps, have felt to some degree at times. What does he teach us about prayer? Why does he pray?

- Jesus prays because he knows that God is sovereign. When we pray, we acknowledge that Someone else has power, even ultimate control, over the events around us.
- Jesus prays because he knows his weakness. When we pray, we realize that we need help.
- Jesus prays because he really wants to do what God knows is best, not what he thinks is best. When we pray, we bypass all the human opinions, human systems and strategies, and human arrogance that tell us how to behave.
- Jesus prays because God is the One he trusts and loves the most. When we pray, we enter into a relationship with Someone whom we can't see but whom we trust more completely than others we can see.

Is that unbelievable or what? Even more illogical: *prayer works.* Not like a computer, with steady, reliable, fixed results. Not like a slot machine, with a lot of investment and occasional jackpots. Not like Santa Claus, with rewards for being good little girls and boys.

Prayer works because God works—always. It's illogical, yes. Oh yes, it's wildly, wonderfully, unpredictably, powerfully, gloriously illogical.

LEADER'S GUIDE

FOCUS

Growing Closer to God:
Serving Others

SCRIPTURE

John 13:1-17

SCAN

Today's meeting introduces the fourth and final of our ways to draw closer to God—through serving other people:
- In Attitude Check, group members picture themselves as fruitful plants.
- In Attitude Question, members discuss their individual "giftedness" and look for ways to use their gifts to serve others.
- Attitude Search examines the story of Jesus washing the disciples' feet.
- In Attitude Adjustment, members take part in a foot-washing ceremony.
- Attitude Exit challenges group members to "practice senseless beauty and random acts of kindness."

STUFF

Bibles
photocopies of today's paper (pp. 117-118), 1 per participant
pens or pencils
sample seed packets
drawing paper
colored felt markers
scissors
basin of *warm* water
towels
chalkboard and chalk or newsprint and marker

1. Attitude Check: I'M A PLANT

Welcome group members. Distribute the sample seed packets for group members

to look at. Note that a picture of the plant appears on one side of the packet, and a description of the plant—its leaves, its flower or fruit, its need for sun, water, etc.—appears on the back side of the packet.

Distribute drawing paper, scissors and colored felt markers. Explain:
- Imagine *yourself* as a plant that grows in someone's garden. Don't say it aloud, but what kind of plant would you be? What kind of flower or fruit would you bear? Would you need lots of sun or a little sun? lots of water or a little water?
- Draw yourself as that plant. Start by cutting out a "seed packet" from paper. Then, on one side, draw the plant you are; on the other side, describe yourself and the conditions in which you grow best.
- Make sure your description explains what you "yield," what special gifts you give to others.

Give group members time to complete their seed packets, then invite volunteers to share what they've drawn and written. Ask members to explain why they've pictured themselves as they did. In particular, use the activity as a way to help group members articulate specific talents and gifts they give to others (their "fruit" or "flowers"), like listening, encouraging, friendship, love and support.

2. Attitude Question: WHAT I CAN GIVE

Invite group members to discuss:
- God gives each of us certain gifts and abilities. What gifts and abilities did we identify as we described ourselves as plants?
- What other gifts and abilities do we have? What do we have to give to others? In what ways has God equipped you to serve others?

- What do you have to give? What are your gifts?
- Why are you given talents? What are they for? How do you use them?
- What are the different ways we can serve in our churches? communities? homes? schools? families?
- How is doing for others doing things for God?
- How do you benefit from serving others?
- How is each individual gifted to serve in unique and different ways?

3. Attitude Search: JOHN 13:1-17

Distribute Bibles and recruit three volunteers to read dramatically John 13:1-17, assigning the parts of *the narrator, Simon Peter* and *Jesus. Stop the reading after verse 12.* Ask:
- Without reading any further, how would *you* answer Jesus' question? Do *we* understand what Jesus has just done to the disciples? What was the message in Jesus' actions?

Let group members discuss their answers, then ask *Jesus* to complete the reading of the passage (vv. 13-17). Discuss:
- In what way do you think Jesus was brought closer to the disciples by washing their feet?
- In what way do you think the disciples were brought closer to Jesus because he washed their feet?

4. Attitude Adjustment: WASHING FEET

Seat group members in a circle, either on chairs or on the floor. Ask members to remove their shoes and socks. Select one person in the circle with whom to begin. Carry the basin of warm water to that person and gently wash his or her feet; do this by holding the person's feet over the basin and scooping water up over the feet with your free hand. Then dry the person's feet with the towel.

Repeat the washing for the next person in the circle, but allow the *first* person to dry the feet of this second person.

Continue around the circle, always letting the previous person in the circle dry the feet of the person whose feet you have just washed. Invite the last person in the circle to wash and dry your feet.

Ask group members to put their shoes and socks back on in silence. When they've finished, ask:
- How did you feel as your feet were washed and dried?
  — In what ways do people "wash our feet"?
  — How do you feel when others serve you?
  — When is being served or helped by others easy? hard? What makes the difference?
  — How can being served or helped by others draw us closer to God?
- How did you feel as you washed and dried someone else's feet?
  — In what ways do we "wash the feet" of others?
  — How do you feel as you serve others?
  — When is serving or helping others easy? hard? What makes the difference?
  — How can serving or helping others draw us closer to God?

5. Attitude Exit: CHALLENGE

Distribute pens or pencils and copies of today's ATTITUDE paper. Ask group members individually to complete the activity Senseless Beauty, Random Kindness, printed in the papers.

When members have finished, regather and invite them to share what they've written in all three spaces in the activity. When all who wish to share have done so, discuss:
- We've had four meetings about growing closer to God.
- Of all the things we've talked about and tried, which has been most meaningful to you?
- What might you do in the future to continue growing closer to God?

a division of
Church Publishing
Incorporated

600 Grant St., #400
Denver, CO 80203
1.800.824.1813

SERVING OTHERS

[ATTITUDE

FOR TEENS BY TEENS

SERVING *by Lori VanDeman*

I've discovered three fundamental parts to my walk with Christ. The first is study—reading the Bible and searching for ways to apply it to everyday life; the second is prayer—building a strong, communicative relationship with God; and the third —and in my opinion the most im- portant—is *serving others*.

Serving others is an outreach of our love for God and our desire to do God's work. Serving results from both prayer and study: in study, the Bible tells us repeatedly that the one who will be first in heaven is also the one who is a servant on earth; in prayer, our constant communication with God motivates us for action. Serving is both a result of Christian life and a stepping stone to bring us closer to Christ.

Serving takes many forms, like working at a soup kitchen, helping a person who has dropped papers in the hall or just holding a door for someone. No matter how simple or complex the deed, the point is to give of yourself for the sake of an- other.

It's easy to incorporate serving into your everyday routine. Look around: you're sure to find opportu- nities to serve. Make each task a prayer and a gift to God, and you'll find that you have lots to give...in joy, peace and love.

WHAT'S IN IT FOR ME? *by Matt Sheen*

What's in it for me?

Why should I throw away my precious time and energy for some- one else when I'm not rewarded for it?

How can I afford to work for oth- ers when there's so much I need to do for myself?

Unfortunately, these are often some of the first questions we ask when we face an opportunity to give of ourselves. In this fast-paced, com- petitive world, we seldom find a place for philanthropy and good deeds.

Yet the Bible tells us to put our faith to work in the service of others: "So it is with faith: if it is alone and includes no actions, then it is dead" (James 2:17). Serving others gives our faith meaning. As we share our gifts and spread hope, our confi- dence in God increases. Our bond with God grows all the stronger as we act more like Jesus.

So with this in mind, we must always strive to treat others as we want to be treated, to live with a good and compassionate heart.

So what's in it for me? Doing what God desires. And a closer rela- tionship with God.

[ATTITUDE

Living the Good News

SENSELESS BEAUTY, RANDOM KINDNESS

Have you seen the bumper sticker that says:

> Practice senseless beauty and random acts of kindness.

Sometimes serving others just doesn't make sense...it just happens, jumping up from inside us to touch someone else's life with unexpected joy.

In this space, write down something that someone did for you that was unexpected and kind:

In this space, write down something that you've done for someone recently...a senseless, surprising, helpful thing:

In this space, write down something you could do for someone this week. What *senseless beauty* could you practice? What *random act of kindness* could you offer?

This meeting's challenge: Do what you've written in the last space above. Serve someone this week.

THE INSIDE STORY

JOHN 13:1-17

See Jesus, who wants to do one last thing to show his friends his love. It must have been something like the urge a parent has to tuck a child in at night—a last kiss, a soft word of reassurance, a caress, a promise of morning. Jesus faces a dark night and knows his friends will also go through a painful, frightening experience. What can he give them?

After their last meal together, he gets up from the table, takes off his nice jacket, wraps an old towel around his waist and begins to untie sandals. Now smell these feet. These are not nice showered feet covered with cotton socks and good shoes that have walked on pavement all day. No...

Jesus gently wipes these feet, which have been covered with nothing but some straps of leather, with his wet towel. He wipes off the dried sweat caked with dust, flecks of manure from the road, toe jam and other such crusty matter. No wonder Peter was so embarrassed. Jesus is their Lord! It's undignified for him to stoop so low.

But Jesus is determined. Not primarily to prove a point or even to set an example, though he does both. First and foremost, his act of service is an act of love. And love goes as low as it needs to, all the way down to the ground.

The point Jesus proves is that love loves to serve. The example Jesus sets is one of love speaking love, not with grand, lofty, admirable words or gestures, but with quiet, humble, generous actions.

A last reminder from the gospels: What Jesus did for his friends that night, he does for you, today, somewhere, somehow. Love reaches out, always.

> Love loves to serve...not with grand, lofty, admirable words or gestures, but with quiet, humble, generous actions.

LEADERS' GUIDE

FOCUS

Questions of Faith:
Does Prayer Really Work?

SCRIPTURE

John 15:1-17

SCAN

Today's meeting invites group members to discuss prayer:
- In Attitude Check, group members roleplay various responses of God to human prayer.
- Attitude Question allows members to ask honest questions about prayer.
- Attitude Search uses Jesus' imagery of the vine to illustrate our connection to God through prayer.
- In Attitude Adjustment, a panel of "Gods" respond to members' prayer requests.
- Attitude Exit invites members to "pray for prayer."

STUFF

Bibles
photocopies of today's paper (pp. 121-122), 1 per participant
pens or pencils
prayer-response cards (see **before the meeting** note)
tape or tacks
chalkboard and chalk or newsprint and marker

Before the meeting copy each of these prayer responses on a separate index card:
- Do it yourself.
- Yes.
- No.
- You selfish little pig!
- I love you too much to grant you that.
- Just wait.
- Consider it done.
- Who cares.

- Get a life.
- Keep at it...you'll get it.
- You've got to be kidding!
- I've got better stuff to do.
- All in due time.
- Do you really need that right now?

1. Attitude Check: NEXT!

Welcome group members and distribute pens or pencils and copies of today's ATTITUDE paper. Ask members to complete the activity The Problem with Prayer, printed in the papers. Share these examples, if needed:
- How can God hear all of our prayers at once?
- How come God doesn't answer my prayers?
- What if two people pray for opposite outcomes?

Recruit a volunteer to play the role of *God*. Ask *God* to sit at the front of the room. Shuffle and give to *God* the stack of prayer-response cards prepared **before the meeting**. Explain:
- One-by-one, you will come forward to stand before *God*. As you approach *God*, *God* will ask, "What can I do for you, my child?"
- You may then state a prayer request to *God*.
- God will answer your request by drawing and reading the top card in God's stack of cards.
- God will then dismiss you by calling out, "Next!" At that point the next group member steps forward to make a request.
- This activity is all in fun; don't ask for serious things.

2. Attitude Question: IS THIS PRAYER?

Discuss:
- The answers given by *God* in the opening activity reflect various views of prayer.

— Which of these answers reflect *your* current view of prayer? Explain.

— Which answers reflect views of prayer with which you disagree? Explain.

● The answers in the opening activity also reflect various understandings of what God is like.

— Which of these answers reflect *your* understanding of God? Explain.

— Which answers reflect understandings of God with which you disagree? Explain.

● How do you think prayer works?

● What do you believe is the purpose of prayer? *("Asking for and receiving things from God," may be a common response. Encourage group members to also think of "establishing a connection with God" or "developing a relationship with God," a theme explored in Attitude Search.)*

● What's the current status of our prayer lives?

— When do we pray?

— For what do we pray?

— In what different ways do we pray?

— What results from our prayers?

Invite volunteers to share the questions about prayer that they wrote in their papers. Lead a discussion using group members' questions. You might also ask:

● Who has also had this question about prayer?

● Who would like to volunteer an answer for this question about prayer?

● How might God answer that question about prayer?

3. Attitude Search: JOHN 15:1-17

Distribute Bibles and ask group members to read silently John 15:1-17. When they have finished their reading, discuss:

● Who is speaking in these verses?

● What do you think Jesus means when he urges us to remain in him? to remain in his love?

● What results from remaining connected to Jesus and Jesus' love?

● In what ways does prayer help us to remain connected to Jesus and to Jesus' love?

Invite group members to review silently these verses and to each choose one verse they particularly like. Ask volunteers to read aloud and explain their choices.

4. Attitude Adjustment: NEXT! TIMES THREE

Recruit three volunteers to roleplay *God*. Take these three volunteers aside and assign each a different role:

● You are the true God, compassionate and loving, who wants what is best for us, even when it may not be what we think we need.

● You are a false God, aloof, detached, distant; you don't really care about us; we annoy you.

● You are a false God, authoritarian and dictatorial, a control freak; you get your kicks from telling us what to do.

Seat the *Gods* at the front of the group, keeping their roles a secret. Invite group members to again come forward, one at a time, to make requests of *God*. Each member chooses which *God* to ask. That *God* then spontaneously answers the request, *speaking from his or her role.*

Discuss:

● How do our three *Gods* differ?

● Which *God* sounds most like *your* God?

● Which method of answering prayer sounds most like prayer as you understand it?

● How, in today's meeting, has your view of prayer changed?

5. Attitude Exit: MOST IMPORTANT PRAYER

Lead group members in a discussion of:

● If we could pray *for prayer,* what would we ask?

Ask a volunteer to write group members' suggestions on chalkboard or newsprint. After several minutes, close by praying:

● All of what we have just written is our prayer to you, God. We want to be connected to you, to your Son Jesus and to your love. *Amen.*

a division of Church Publishing Incorporated

600 GRANT ST., #400
DENVER, CO 80203
1.800.824.1813

DOES PRAYER REALLY WORK?

ATTITUDE
FOR TEENS BY TEENS

PRAYER by Rachel Gluckstern

god?
are you listening?

*when two or more are gathered
in my name
i am in the midst of them*

i'm all alone god
i'm scared
help me

*god helps those
who helps themselves*

fear is blinding me
where do I turn?
verses do not reassure me
friends cannot comfort

*a time for sorrow
a time for joy*

when will my time come?
i'm so cold
so cold
empty
a void within me

filled with the Holy Spirit

i've found god
small bit of warmth
seeping into my frozen heart
connection
communion
amen

PRAYER: WHAT WORKS FOR ME by Rachel Gluckstern

Speaking to God is a private and personal part of our spiritual lives. Prayer helps us reconnect all the different pieces of ourselves. Prayer grounds and centers us. Prayer is a way to communicate directly with God.

Some people, however, use prayer like an ATM card or a 1-800-request line. They no longer use prayer to revere God or to communicate with God, but as a way to ask for favors. Worse yet, many of these people base their faith on whether or not God grants them what they ask for. Does God hand out answers like candy bars?

I'm not sure if you would even call what I do *prayer*. I meditate, and in meditation strive for connection or communion with God. I look to touch the divine, a force that I believe binds us all together. I believe God wants me to make wise decisions and chose the right paths in my life, and my communion with God gives me the confidence that this is happening. I don't pray to get stuff out of God like a cosmic vending machine but to *be with God*, knowing and experiencing God's presence within me.

I also believe prayer is the place to praise and worship God, to feel the awe of something bigger than I am...bigger than my problems, bigger even than all of creation. And I feel great gratitude to God and always take the opportunity in prayer to thank God for all that God has done for us.

I urge you to use prayer to connect with God in whatever way works for you. In a world full of illusions and uncertainties, maintaining a spiritual connection is vital to us all. What's *your* way to pray?

© Copyright 2000
Living the Good News
a division of Church Publishing Incorporated
600 Grant Street
Suite 400
Denver, CO 80203
1 (800) 824-1813

Graphic Design & Illustration:
Carolyn Klass

ATTITUDE

Living the Good News

THE PROBLEM WITH PRAYER

What questions do you have about prayer?

Today's meeting will offer you an opportunity to ask the really tough questions about prayer. You may get some answers, or you may end up with more questions, but one thing is for sure—you'll discover you're not alone in struggling with the "prayer puzzle."

Use this space to write down some of the questions you've always had about prayer. You'll have a chance to ask, compare and discuss questions later in the meeting.

THE INSIDE STORY

JOHN 15:1-17

Often when we ask if prayer works, a variety of images spring to mind. Perhaps we see a large warehouse full of good things, with God in charge of the inventory. We order online, God processes it, and BOOM, order shipped and delivery promised in 24 hours.

Or maybe we're still into Santa Claus, who sees who's naughty and nice, and who wants to hear our wish lists. Or maybe we're into high-tech prayer. A computer perhaps. Click on the right icon and zip-bang, there it is. Or even a slot machine, where there aren't any predictable results, but somewhere someone will someday hit a jackpot.

Well, if any of those images are your idea of prayer, then no, prayer doesn't "work." When you ask if something works, you first have to know what it is and what it's designed to do. If you think a toaster is supposed to dry your hair, asking whether it works or not is beside the point. When we ask if prayer works, we need to know what prayer is.

Jesus gives the true image of prayer: a grapevine. Jesus is the vine; God is the gardener; we are the branches; letting the life of the vine flow through us is prayer; the events of our lives are God's pruning efforts to make our prayers more fruitful; grapes are the "answers" to prayer.

Now to live in Jesus is to talk to Jesus, to listen to Jesus, to love Jesus, and all of that is part of prayer. But ultimately, prayer is not the words you say, it's who you are. If you're living in Jesus, you are praying whether you're playing basketball, making your bed, going to class, watching a movie, whatever. We can do those things without Jesus, but Jesus tells us that when we don't remain in him our prayer is interrupted. But if we remain in him, then prayer happens all the time. Prayer is our relationship with Jesus.

And the fruit? Jesus promises that those who remain in him will bear fruit. Their prayers "work." Sometimes we'll bear fruit that we didn't expect, or we won't bear fruit that we did expect. But when we ask in Jesus' name, we can be sure that our deepest desires, which are found in the love of Jesus, will be granted.

LEADERS' GUIDE

FOCUS

Questions of Faith:
Do Faith and Science Conflict?

SCRIPTURE

Genesis 1:1–2:4a

SCAN

Today's meeting examines the potential conflict between faith and science:

- Attitude Check invites group members to create a new animal, both "scientifically" and "religiously."
- In Attitude Adjustment, members discuss the perceived conflict between science and faith.
- Attitude Search explores the classic "science vs. faith" scripture, the story of creation.
- Attitude Adjustment asks members to decide who created a variety of items, God or science?
- In Attitude Exit, members pray the words of a hymn.

STUFF

Bibles
photocopies of today's paper (pp. 125-126), 1 per participant
pens or pencils
index cards, 1 per participant
2 bags of pipe cleaners
chalkboard and chalk or newsprint and marker

Before the meeting cut 10 pictures from newspapers or magazines and glue them to a sheet of poster board, numbering the pictures 1 to 10:

1. nuclear explosion
2. cordless or cellular telephone
3. beeper or pager
4. weight lifter
5. gold ring
6. syringe
7. puppy or kitten
8. tree
9. any object clearly made from wood, like a table or chair
10. gun

1. Attitude Check: THE CREATORS

Welcome group members and distribute pens or pencils and index cards. Ask each group member to write down the "problems" that he or she has with science and faith, or science and the Bible. If necessary, share these examples:

- Can we believe in both creation and evolution?
- Can I trust both medicine and miracles?

Ask members to save these cards for later in the meeting.

Divide participants into two groups. Label one group *The People of Faith* and the other group *The People of Science*. Give each group a bag of pipe cleaners.

Offer these directions to *The People of Faith*:

- Your task is to create an entirely new animal using your pipe cleaners.
- The only direction is that you must create this animal "religiously," whatever you think that means.

Give these directions to *The People of Science*:

- Your task is to create an entirely new animal using your pipe cleaners.
- The only direction is that you must create this animal "scientifically," whatever you think that means.

Gives groups time to create their animals, struggling, if they do, to understand what it might mean to create "religiously" or to create "scientifically."

Bring the groups together and ask them to show their new animals and to explain

ATTITUDE FOR TEENS BY TEENS

the process they went through to create it, either "religiously" or "scientifically."

Note: If groups have been immobilized by the task of doing their job either "religiously" or "scientifically," ask:
● What did you think creating "religiously" (or "scientifically") meant?
● How did you think your assignment differed from that of the other group?

Discuss:
● What's the difference between our animals?
● What's the difference in the *process* we went through to create our animals?
● How did God create animals, scientifically or religiously?

2. Attitude Question: GOD AND SCIENCE

Discuss:
● What is God's role in science?
● In what ways is your faith challenged by what you know or are learning about science and technology? How have you known the faith of others to be challenged by science or technology?
● What questions can science answer that faith cannot? What questions can faith answer that science cannot?
● Respond to each of these statements:
— All truth is God's truth.
— When the Bible and science contradict, God wins.
— God creates and science discovers.

Invite volunteers to share the questions they wrote at the beginning of the meeting. Lead a discussion using group members' questions.

3. Attitude Search: GENESIS 1:1–2:4a

Distribute Bibles and invite volunteers to read aloud Genesis 1:1–2:4a, each volunteer reading a paragraph or two. Discuss:
● How has this story been a source of the conflict for science and the Bible?

● For yourself, how have you reconciled the conflict between evolution and creation?
— What middle ground have some people found between a "science-less" understanding of creation or a "God-less" understanding of evolution?
— In what ways might God have been active in evolution? In what ways might the principles of evolution have been active in creation?
● What other examples of potential conflict between science and scripture (or science and faith) can you think of?

4. Attitude Adjustment: WHO CREATES WHAT?

Distribute copies of today's ATTITUDE paper. Direct group members attention to the list of numbers found in Of God or Science?, printed in the papers. Display the poster prepared **before the meeting**. Explain:
● For each item on the poster, in the appropriate space on your paper, write whether you think that item is something that comes from God or something that comes from science.

Allow several minutes, then regather and tally members' responses, perhaps on the poster itself. On some items you may have complete agreement, but for many you will have disagreement. As appropriate, ask:
● Why do we disagree on this item?
● To what extent was this a joint venture between God and science?
● If this was created primarily by science, did God also have it in mind? Did God intend it? Explain.

5. Attitude Exit: GOD OF CONCRETE

Direct group members' attention to the words of the hymn "God of Concrete, God of Steel," printed in the papers. Read this hymn in unison as today's closing prayer.

a division of
Church Publishing
Incorporated

600 Grant St., #400
Denver, CO 80203
1.800.824.1813

DO FAITH AND SCIENCE CONFLICT?

ATTITUDE

FOR TEENS BY TEENS

THE CONTEST OF FAITH AND SCIENCE
by Nate Fandel

Many years ago a great argument arose on Mount Olympus. The thunder of the dispute echoed through the valleys and over the peaks. It was a debate between Faith and Science, and it lasted, in human terms, many lifetimes.

Faith had invited the confrontation when she realized that humanity, for the first time, dared doubt her importance, dared doubt the importance of the sacred and divine. Where once people explained even the tiniest items of daily life as acts of Faith, they now dismissed daily miracles as simple acts of this new thing called Science. The mystery disappeared, the miraculous and holy became mechanical and common.

Science was an attractive deity, most knowledgeable in the workings of the physical world. Science gave people ideas...*progress*, they called it...things like genetic engineering and penicillin and people traveling to the moon. Science was happy, really, for people understood him and communicated in his language.

People lost interest in Faith and traded her for Science.

So Faith invited Science to Mount Olympus for a discussion.

They met one afternoon for a talk. Faith explained that without her there would be no Science, nor, for that matter, any need for him. Science answered that without him, the women and men whom Faith had created would be no different than the animals, never progressing further in the work she had intended for them. Faith asserted that women and men had been given reason, and that this already separated them from the animals. Science rebutted that it was humanity's ability to reason that created him in the first place. On and on they argued, always louder, never getting anywhere.

Finally, Faith and Science decided that the debate could only be settled with a competition, a contest to prove who had the real power. It would be determined by a test. A date was set, and both prepared...

To be continued in the next paper...

FAITH VS. SCIENCE?
by Jerry Berg

It is believed by many people that faith and science cannot exist together. Most who believe this are themselves at what seem to be opposite poles, one group saying that only faith is legitimate, the other saying that only science is real.

I don't agree. I think science and faith can exist together.

God created scientific minds. God gave humans the ability to think and be creative. Creativity is the basis for all scientific exploration and discovery; reason is the method by which we test and prove our hypotheses. The first scientific experiment was the creation of the world, and that experiment runs on. God created science.

What about the debate over creation vs. evolution? I think the argument is pointless. "The world was created in seven days," say the creationists. But how long were those days? The sun supposedly wasn't created until the fourth day, so when did the first day begin? I assume it's on God's clock, and since God is forever, who knows how big the chunks are when God's measuring time.

Who was around keeping a stopwatch on God anyway? The point of
(continued on page 2)

© Copyright 2000
Living the Good News
a division of Church Publishing Incorporated
600 Grant Street
Suite 400
Denver, CO 80203
1 (800) 824-1813

Graphic Design & Illustration:
Carolyn Klass

OF GOD OR SCIENCE?

FAITH VS. SCIENCE (continued from page 1)

Everything we know about God was written down by humans, humans who struggled to understand the complexity of God, just like we

the story of creation is that God was in charge, and that however it was done, it was impressive.

do. We catch glimpses of God in their story, just as we learn more about God through the wonders of physics, genetics and other scientific works. We have our whole lives to explore the mystery of God, so let's not rule out any avenue—let's embrace both faith and science.

GOD OF CONCRETE

Francis Westerbrook, b. 1903

God of concrete, God of steel,
God of piston and of wheel,
God of pylon, God of steam,
God of girder and of beam,
God of atom, God of mine,
All the world of power is Thine!

Lord of cable, Lord of rail,
Lord of motorway and mail,
Lord of rocket, Lord of flight,
Lord of soaring satellite,
Lord of lightning's livid line,
All the world of speed is Thine!

Lord of science, Lord of art,
God of map and graph and chart,
Lord of physics and research,
Word of Bible, faith of Church,
Lord of sequence and design,
All the world of truth is Thine!

God whose glory fills the earth,
Gave the universe its birth,
Loosed the Christ with Easter's might,
Saves the world from evil's blight,
Claims mankind by grace divine,
All the world of love is Thine!

THE INSIDE STORY

GENESIS 1:1–2:4a

Either we came from monkeys or God created Adam and Eve. Either the universe is expanding matter or God spoke. Either the world is billions of years old or God created everything in six days.

These seem to be our choices when it comes to science and our faith. Some want more options, like none of the above or all of the above. But any of these answers seem to miss the point altogether.

Do faith and science conflict? Yes, if they're trying to answer the same questions. No, if they're answering different questions.

Look at the creation story. It gives a blow-by-blow account of the creation of the world that doesn't come close to the explanations that the scientists give.

But what questions is the Bible account trying to answer? These are some of them: Where did we come from? Why are we here? Is there a God? What is our relationship with creation? What is our destiny? Who is in charge of the universe? What kind of God do we believe in?

And the scientists ask: How did we get here? What's our world made of? What kind of creatures are we? What's the universe like? How does the universe work?

Now of course there are scientists who try to answer the biblical questions, and there are Christians who try to make the Bible answer the scientific questions. Sometimes the exchange of information is helpful, and sometimes it's not.

A lot of times scientists are wrong. Every new generation of science has disproved pet theories from the generation before and has come up with new explanations, some which will be shown to be true and some which will be refuted. And sometimes our religious beliefs are wrong. Our faith must always grapple with science.

Do they conflict? No. Concur? No. Cooperate? Yes.

LEADERS' GUIDE

FOCUS

Questions of Faith:
Do Miracles Really Happen?

SCRIPTURE

John 6:1-13, 25-33

SCAN

Today's meeting explores the nature of miracles:
- In Attitude Check, group members respond to a report of a real-life miracle.
- Attitude Question offers members an opportunity to voice both their confidence in and questions about miracles.
- Group members explore a biblical miracle story in Attitude Search.
- In Attitude Adjustment, members role-play a miraculous healing.
- Attitude Exit invites members to identify the miraculous in everyday life.

STUFF

Bibles
photocopies of today's paper (pp. 129-130), 1 per participant
pens or pencils
chalkboard and chalk or newsprint and marker

1. Attitude Check: MIRACLE STORY

Welcome group members and explain that today's topic is miracles. Invite members to offer definitions of a miracle. Record their suggestions on chalkboard or newsprint. Share this definition:
- A miracle is an event in which the usual laws of nature appear to be overruled or suspended, often attributed to the action of God.

Distribute pens or pencils and copies of today's ATTITUDE paper. Invite group members to complete the activity The Mystery of Miracles, printed in the papers.

When group members have finished, invite them to read silently the story The Healing of Sean, also printed in the papers. Discuss:
- What's going on in this story?
- If you were asked to explain how Sean was healed, what would you say?

2. Attitude Question: THE NATURE OF MIRACLES

Invite group members to share other modern-day miracle stories they have heard about. Discuss:
- To what do you attribute these modern-day miracles?
- To what extent do you believe these miracles are the direct work of God? To what extent do you believe miracles might be the result of medicine? technology? nature? human will?
- If God is working these miracles today, what do you think God's purpose is?

Invite group members to think more broadly about miracles:
- What other "miracles" do you witness in the world around you, beyond the apparent intervention of God to save lives or heal people?

If group members need help thinking of ideas, you might suggest the miracles of childbirth, friendship, a sunrise, etc.— any circumstance that brings a response of wonder and an acknowledgment of God's greatness. After members have offered ideas, ask:
- What makes these things miraculous to us?
- In what ways might we benefit from living with eyes open to the miraculous around us?

ATTITUDE FOR TEENS BY TEENS

● What can we do to help open our eyes to everyday miracles?

Invite volunteers to share the questions written in their papers at the beginning of the meeting. Lead a discussion using group members' questions. Helpful questions could include:
● Who has also had this question about miracles?
● Who would like to volunteer an answer for this question?

3. Attitude Search: JOHN 6:1-13, 25-33

Distribute Bibles and ask group members to turn together to John 6:1-13. Recruit four volunteers to read these verses dramatically, assigning the parts of *Jesus, Philip, Andrew* and *the narrator*. Discuss:
● What do you think of this miracle? Do you believe in this miracle? Why or why not?
● If you believe in this miracle, what was Jesus' purpose in performing it?
● If you doubt this miracle, what do you think is John's purpose in including it in this story of Jesus? What is John telling us?

Invite group members to recall other miracles from the Bible. Discuss:
● To what extent do you believe these miracles were the direct work of God? the result of natural causes? the result of human intervention?
● What do you think was the purpose of these miracles in the Bible? What was the purpose for those who witnessed them? for those of us who read about them?

Ask *the narrator* to read aloud John 6:25-33, with all other group members taking the part of *the people* in verses 25, 28 and 30-31. Discuss:
● Jesus knew that people had trouble understanding his miracles. According to verses 26-27, what problem does Jesus see arising?

● The people refer to another miracle in verse 31. What is that miracle? (See Exodus 16:4.)
● According to Jesus in verses 27, 29 and 32-33, what is the purpose of his ministry, including his miracles?

4. Attitude Adjustment: CONSULTATION

Recruit volunteers for a roleplay, two to play *patients* and three to play *doctors*. Lay both *patients* on tables, couches or on the floor. Explain:
● These two *patients* have identical diseases.
● These are the doctors treating both patients, and they've given both patients the same treatment. They've also pronounced the same diagnosis for both: *death!*
● *This* patient *(point to one volunteer)... dies!*
● *This* patient *(point to the other volunteer) ...is suddenly and completely cured!*
● It's a miracle!
● Let's hear what the doctors have to say.

Let the doctors discuss the case. You may help them by asking:
● Doctors, what happened? Why did one live and one die?
● Doctors, how will you explain this to the hospital's board of directors?

Ask other group members to join the discussion, while inviting the volunteers (including the healed *patient*) to stay in their roles.

5. Attitude Exit: TODAY'S MIRACLES

Gather group members in a circle. Go around the circle, giving each member an opportunity to share one "everyday miracle" he or she has experienced in the past week. Close by praying:
● God of miracles, open our eyes, hearts and minds to see you working in our lives every day. *Amen.*

a division of Church Publishing Incorporated

600 GRANT ST., #400 DENVER, CO 80203 1.800.824.1813

DO MIRACLES REALLY HAPPEN?

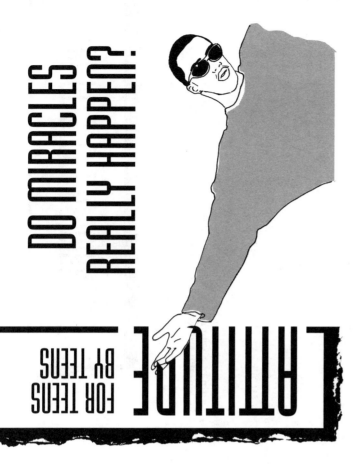

ATTITUDE
BY TEENS FOR TEENS

THE CONTEST OF FAITH AND SCIENCE by Nate Faudel

(continued from the previous paper)

The date for the big contest between Faith and Science arrived. The two great beings were edgy and anxious. They wanted the games to begin. The contest? Who could perform the most amazing miracle.

Faith set out with her people to find a suitable, stunning miracle. "I know what I want to do," said Faith in a whisper. "I want to bring a mortal back to life."

Science gathered with his people. "I know what will win the contest," said Science confidentially to his helpers. "I will give life to a dead human."

Without realizing it, both Faith and Science placed themselves in the same remote village in South America, recently hit by a terrible earthquake. Faith stood in a crowded makeshift emergency room set up in a tent at one end of the village; Science huddled in a corner of a crumbling clinic at the opposite end of the village.

Faith waited as an injured child struggled to take her last breaths. The child's father sobbed nearby. "Have faith, mortal father," sighed Faith. The child died. The father wailed. Faith watched. The doctors continued working, trying to revive the lifeless body. Finally, as the

(continued on page 2)

THE HEALING OF SEAN

In early August of 1994, 15-year-old Sean began having headaches. At first they just annoyed him, but slowly grew more painful and frequent. By late August, his head hurt almost constantly, so Sean's parents took him to see a doctor.

The doctor recommended a series of tests. The results were devastating: Sean had a brain tumor. Even worse, the tumor was located deep within Sean's brain, and surgery was impossible.

The doctors treated Sean with a combination of drugs and radiation. Sean lost all his hair, had trouble eating or sleeping and dropped about ¼ of his body weight. Then he returned for more tests. Had the tumor receded? Was Sean going to be okay?

No. With great sadness the doctors informed Sean and his parents that the tumor had continued to grow. Things looked hopeless, they said. They would continue treatment, but they didn't expect it to work.

Sean's parents wouldn't accept the prognosis. Though they had been praying all along for Sean to be healed, now they expanded their efforts. Their church rallied around them, keeping a 24-hour prayer vigil for Sean.

Sean's parents hired a therapist to help Sean deal with his pain and fear. The therapist taught Sean how to visualize his own healing, how to relax and call on God for strength and on his body's own healing powers to fight the cancer.

When Sean went in for his next checkup, around Thanksgiving, his headaches had stopped. Tests showed that the tumor had shrunk by over ⅔. The doctors were amazed. Sean's parents were overjoyed. And Sean, oddly, was barely surprised.

Everyone kept praying. Sean kept seeing his therapist. The doctors continued Sean's medication.

When Sean was again checked shortly after the new year, doctors found no trace of the cancer.

Was it a miracle?

© Copyright 2000
Living the Good News
a division of Church Publishing Incorporated
600 Grant Street
Suite 400
Denver, CO 80203
1 (800) 824-1813

Graphic Design & Illustration:
Carolyn Klass

ATTITUDE

Living the Good News

THE MYSTERY OF MIRACLES

What questions do you have about miracles?

Today's meeting will offer you an opportunity to ask any questions you'd like about miracles. You may get some answers, or you may end up with more questions, but one thing is for sure—you'll find that other people in the group have questions about miracles, too.

Use this space to write down some of the questions you've always had about miracles. You'll have a chance to ask, compare and discuss questions later in the meeting.

THE CONTEST (continued from page 1)

judges from Olympus watched. Faith waved her mighty arm. The child coughed, choked and started to cry. She sat up and reached for her father. "It's a miracle," said the judges from Mount Olympus.

Meanwhile, across the devastation of the village, Science watched as dust-covered stretcher-bearers, bandannas covering their mouths and noses, brought a young man into the clinic. A harried nurse ripped open the man's shirt and listened at his heart. "Nothing," she proclaimed. "Too late for this one."

"Maybe not," thought Science, waving a mighty arm. "Maybe not," said a doctor, stepping to the table. Within seconds the young man was attached to a variety of tubes and machines, one to breathe for him, one to circulate his blood, one to monitor his heart, another to watch his blood pressure. The right medicine, the proper stimulation—all the best that Science could bring—was brought to play. Science watched, holding his breath, and did not breathe again until the man began to breathe on his own. The judges watched from Mount Olympus; "It's a miracle," they said.

The judges declared the contest a tie. "Faith creates the system," they declared. "Science explains the system. Faith is the first master, Science the second. What Faith has done first, Science does again with the tools Faith provides. Without Faith, there is no Science."

Faith and Science both found satisfaction with the results of the contest.

THE INSIDE STORY

JOHN 6:1-13, 25-33

Yes and no. Yes, miracles happen if you have eyes to see them. No, miracles do not happen if you do not have seeing eyes.

A miracle, any event that interrupts the normal laws of nature to reveal God's presence, is a mystery. It throws out of kilter all our expectations, contradicts all our experience, discounts all our information about the world. Miracles make a lot of people uncomfortable, and so they try to control such mysteries with explanations or objections or refutations.

The skeptics say: The laws of the universe are unbreakable. Objects cannot fall up; dead people cannot breathe; a human being cannot walk on water; bread does not fall from the skies. These kinds of happenings are illogical and therefore impossible.

But the eyes of faith say: Yes, such events are unreasonable, but there is truth that lies beyond reason's reach. Reason is not the only way we discern reality. Reason does not love or sacrifice or weep or laugh. Miracles are God-events, happenings that momentarily rip open a hole in the fabric, and the reason, of this world and let us see God's presence.

The skeptics say: Miracles are simply natural events for which we have not yet discovered the explanation. Miracles are like nature's tricks that only await a revelation of the magician's trade secrets.

The eyes of faith say: God is busy in our world every day. The Incarnation, God's ultimate interruption, is not a biological phenomenon that may one day be duplicated through technological advances. If God is bold enough to become a human being, anything can happen.

Jesus isn't surprised by skepticism. He feeds over 5,000 hungry people with a sack lunch and has leftovers for nights to come. But the very next day, the people are back in his face, demanding more. More food. More proof. More miracles. Did they see a miracle or not? Yes...and no.

LEADERS' GUIDE

ATTITUDE FOR TEENS BY TEENS

FOCUS

Questions of Faith:
Is There an Afterlife?

SCRIPTURE

Mark 12:18-27

SCAN

Today's meeting looks at heaven and the afterlife:

- In Attitude Check, group members sketch their ideas of heaven.
- Attitude Question invites members to discuss their beliefs and opinions about life after death.
- In Attitude Search, members expand on Jesus' understanding of what happens in the next life.
- Small groups create posters illustrating "the ideal afterlife" in Attitude Adjustment.
- In Attitude Exit members pray a prayer for those who question.

STUFF

Bibles
photocopies of today's paper (pp. 133-134), 1 per participant
pens or pencils
index cards
drawing paper
drawing pencils
chalkboard and chalk or newsprint and marker
poster board, 1 sheet per every 3-4 participants
colored felt markers
tape or tacks

1. Attitude Check: HEAVEN SKETCHES

Welcome group members and ask each group member to write down on index cards the "problems" (if any) that he or she has with the concept of heaven or the afterlife, for example: Is heaven real? Will some people not make it to heaven?

Distribute drawing pencils and drawing paper. Ask each group member quickly to sketch his or her view of heaven.

After 5-10 minutes, gather and invite members to show and explain their drawings to other members of the group. Ask:

- What similarities do our drawings have? what differences?
- Which of our drawings represent a conventional view of heaven? an unconventional or surprising view?

2. Attitude Question: THE AFTERLIFE

Invite group members to discuss:

- From what different sources have we gotten our views of heaven and the afterlife?
- Many different ideas of heaven have been suggested by people in our group:
  — Which do you personally believe?
  — Which do you doubt?
  — Do you believe in heaven? in hell? in purgatory?
- What do we understand to be the *biblical* view of heaven and the afterlife?
- What alternative afterlife views do you know of?
- What difference does belief in an afterlife make in our lives?
  — What purpose does the afterlife serve in your life?
  — How much does knowledge of an afterlife motivate your actions in *this* life?
  — How might you live differently if you were certain there was no afterlife?
- Respond to this expression: *They're so heavenly-minded that they're no earthly good.*

- Is it necessary to believe in heaven in order to get there?

Invite volunteers to share the questions they wrote on their index cards at the beginning of the meeting. Lead a discussion using group members' questions. Helpful questions could include:
- Who has also had this question about heaven or the afterlife?
- Who would like to volunteer an answer for this question?
- If God were here with us in person, how might God answer that question about the afterlife?

3. Attitude Search: MARK 12:18-27

Distribute Bibles and divide participants into smaller groups of 3-4 members each. Offer groups these directions:
- With the members of your small group, read aloud Mark 12:18-27. You could read in unison, ask a volunteer to read aloud or take turns reading verses.
- After your reading, discuss everything you learn about the afterlife from these verses.
- Be ready to share your findings when we regather.

After 5-10 minutes of discussion, gather groups and ask each group to report on its discussion. Record group members' observations about the afterlife on chalkboard or newsprint. Discuss:
- The Bible's references to heaven, though frequent, don't give us a clear picture of what life after death will be like. Many images of the afterlife are highly symbolic.
- We do expect heaven to be a place of peace, joy, wholeness and beauty, a place where we will have intimacy with God and will worship God, a place of final understanding of many things that remain mysteries now.
- What do these additional Bible verses suggest to us about heaven?

— Matthew 5:11-12
— 2 Corinthians 5:1-5
— Revelation 21:1-4, 22–22:5
- What do *you* hope to find in heaven?

4. Attitude Adjustment: DESIGN-AN-AFTERLIFE

Ask participants to return to the small groups of Attitude Search. Distribute a sheet of poster board to each group. Make available the felt markers.

Ask each group to design and create a poster showing its view of the "ideal afterlife." Explain:
- If it were up to the members of your group, what would heaven be like? What would it look like? feel like? smell like? sound like?
- Who else would be there?
- How would you spend your time? What activities do you hope to find in heaven?
- What will you want to say to God? ask God?

After 10-15 minutes of discussion and drawing, gather groups and invite volunteers from each group to show and explain their posters. Discuss:
- Which ideas sound particularly good to us?
- Which of our groups do we think has presented the *best* idea of heaven?

Tape or tack the completed posters to a wall of the meeting space to enjoy in future weeks.

5. Attitude Exit: A QUESTIONER'S PRAYER

Distribute copies of today's ATTITUDE paper. Ask group members to turn together to A Prayer for Those Who Question, printed in the papers.

Pray this prayer in unison, or invite a volunteer to pray the prayer aloud for the group.

a division of
Church Publishing
Incorporated

600 Grant St., #400
Denver, CO 80203
1.800.824.1813

IS THERE AN AFTERLIFE?

ATTITUDE
FOR TEENS BY TEENS

WHAT LIES BEYOND?

by Rachel Gluckstern

Life's greatest mystery? *What happens to us after we die. What happens to us after we die.* Is there an afterlife? Is there nothingness? Do we reincarnate? What *really* happens?

Most Christians believe in the concept of heaven. Many also believe in hell. These beliefs are also shared by the Islamic faith.

Heaven, of course, is reserved for the faithful. But there is confusion about who gets there and why. Some Christians say that only those who profess faith in Jesus Christ will be welcomed in heaven. Others say heaven will be the place of those who are "good," whose behavior merits salvation. But *good* of course,

is defined differently by different people. For one group of Christians, behaviors a, b and c make one truly "good"; another group could care less about a, b and c, but demand that believers follow x, y and z.

Some faiths teach reincarnation as part of afterlife belief. In reincarnation, a person is repeatedly reborn until they are released from the cycle of life. Reincarnation is a way to live your life over and over again until you get it right.

The afterlife is the greatest enigma. We can't go there, spend

(continued on page 2)

REPENT! THE END IS NEAR!

by Nate Fandel

Above the noise of the crowd I heard a cry, a cry of desperation and anger. The closer I drew to the subway entrance, the clearer I heard the words: "...end is near...repent..." He said it over and over again. "Repent! The end is near!" As the escalator dragged me down into the dark station, I got my first glimpse of the pessimistic news-bearer—a man of about 35, dressed in a robe, monk-like, tall and thin, holding a sign bearing the same message, "Repent! The end is near!" I couldn't connect him to any one religion.

"My ignorant young friend, you have much to learn and you may have only moments to learn it. Death could come at any moment. You have not lived a full life, nor have you been everything you have wanted to be. If you begin now you may at least die trying. If you do not, than you may die knowing you didn't even try!" He had said all of this in one quick, breathless rush. He took a deep breath and pointed at me, saying, louder, *"Do you know what awaits you in the afterlife?"*

I was so taken back by his speech and drama that the only think I could think of to say was, "Nope."

He continued. "Lead the best life that you can. Try. Seek. Strive. Pursue. Persevere. Therein lies your reward. If you do not care or do not try, then you will damned from this moment onward. Change now. Turn. Repent from laziness and complacency. Be a model. Lead others. Make this world better, holier, safer, more loving. Repent and begin your new life!"

Suddenly, as quickly as he had focused on me moments before, he turned away and begin chanting his refrain, over and over, "Repent! The end is near!" The escalator continued pulling people down from the street above. I tried to thank him, but he seemed not to hear.

I walked on toward the platform to catch the 25 uptown.

He spotted me in the crowd, and I was drawn to him. Looking down at me he repeated , "Repent! The end is near!"

"What?" I asked.

ATTITUDE

Living The Good News

A PRAYER FOR THOSE WHO QUESTION

God,

We are at one time
  both a people of faith
  and a people of doubts.
We wonder about so many things:
  prayer,
  science,
  miracles,
  the afterlife...
  these are just a few.
Help us to understand
  that it's okay to doubt,
  that we can believe
  with all sorts of doubt.
Help us to trust
  when we cannot be certain,
  for this,
  in the end,
  is faith.
Amen.

WHAT LIES BEYOND? (continued from page 1)

some time studying it, taking pictures and making notes, and then come back to talk about it. By the time you really understand it, you're there for good.

Our beliefs in the afterlife are powerful, and for many, they guide their behavior in this life. But proof? It has to wait until we die.

What's really beyond life in this world?

THE INSIDE STORY

MARK 12:18-27

Jesus is anything but politically correct. How many people today have the nerve to respond to someone's religious convictions as Jesus does in today's gospel: "How wrong you are!....You are completely wrong!" Whoa. Pretty brazen.

The Sadducees, a Jewish sect or denomination, believe strongly that there is no resurrection from the dead, no future life, no soul, no last judgment. If they were around today, we might give them some leeway: That's their perspective, their version of the truth, their sincere belief; we gotta respect them.

Not Jesus. Nope. He doesn't crusade, he doesn't attack, he doesn't smear; but when asked, he is direct. Jesus does not want anyone to be mistaken about the afterlife. The dead will rise to new life, a life unlike this one in many ways, but life all the same. God is the God of the living, not of the dead.

Perhaps Jesus' answer is blunt because the question is so calculating. The Sadducees' question is closed, put out as a way of proving their point; it's not a legitimate question that welcomes an honest answer. They ask Jesus one of those situation questions that pushes God's law past its intended limits so that it appears ridiculous. They pose the question, using the logic of this world to demonstrate the impossibility of any other.

Jesus tells them that their mistake comes from their ignorance of scripture and their blindness to the power of God. Both the Old Testament and the New are full of references to a coming judgment, a coming life, a coming joy that lies on the other side of death. There is an age to come, Jesus says, and this life is only the rehearsal.

Get ready. It's there, waiting for you. Jesus' post-death experience, his afterlife, will become ours. Do you want it?

Scripture Index

Theme Index